Ginie's Patchwork Exercise Book II

A Project and Inspiration Book

Publishing company: BERGTOR VERLAG GmbH, Grünstadt, Germany
Publisher: Astrid Reck
Graphics: Barbara Klotz
Cover Design: Ginie Curtze
Interior Design: Astrid Reck
Title Quilt: Ginie Curtze
Translator: Andy Curtze
Layout: Satz & Service, Hildegard Pauluweit, Filderstadt, Germany
Printed by: AALEXX Druck GmbH, Germany
© 2004 by Ginie Curtze
ISBN 3-937703-01-2

Contents

Projects

Essays

Extra courses

I would like to thank my quilting friends for their willingness to sew and quilt works that have been inspiration and examples for my Exercise Book II. The wonderful results speak for themselves.

Thank you, dear
Rosi Behlke, Neustrelitz
Katharina Clausen, Constance
Cécile Curtze-Bellmas, Barcelona
Heike Dressler, Gunzenhausen
Anne E. Foerster, Kenzingen
Doris Gehri, Switzerland
Willi Gottsmann, Constance
Renate Haupt, Hamm
Dagmar Huber, Donaueschingen
Jutta Jahrsen, Stuttgart (Beehive Store)
Barbara Malanowski-Casty, Scharans, Switzerland
Barbara May, Paderborn (Barbara's Rainbow)
Monika Pohl, Stuttgart
Eli Thomae, Germaringen (textile studio)
Network-Quilterinnen, international group
Bettina Weber, Viernheim
Pia Welsch, Homburg/Saar

Photos by Gisela Gerstmeier, Constance

Preface

In my first book, the Exercise Book 1, I spoke to you of my love for patchwork and quilting. We learned about patterns, their origins and meanings, about colour and design, and we savoured a few morsels of wisdom about patchwork and quilting.

In 1984, I had the idea to produce metal templates with seam allowance markings. My guiding thought was to make a solid "tool" that allowed for easy and rational cutting of the traditional patterns, leaving more time for the creative part of design. The seam allowances were always the same, so the different templates could be easily interchanged into new patterns like a jigsaw puzzle. The rotary cutter came along just at the right time! Frequently asked question: "Will the blade become dull if I catch the edge of the template while cutting?" I can happily answer "no" to that one – the edges of the templates are designed so that they will not dull your rotary cutter.

If I think back on the past 20 years I can say that with this "simplified" method of cutting, I was able to reach thousands of women who rediscovered their love for patchwork and took it to further levels. For this reason, it is very important to me to present not only my own work, but also that of many of my quilting friends, who have worked sheer magic with the templates.

Don't you agree that sometimes you see many different ideas along a similar theme, and then you become inspired and dream up your own version? I like seeing different expositions around the world in that frame of mind, and if I can discover a trend, I try to think of a simple way of adapting it to my templates. Thus, for example, the Flic-Flac came into existance with its new angles or the Mirror-Mambo. Mirror techniques were first successfully introduced by Jinny Beyer in 1964, she created her own fabric line for them. Later B. Reynolds in her book "Stack and Whack" and Gail Valentine in "Mirror Manipulations" picked up the technique again. There wasn't a quilt expo without at least one example. After its introduction here, the Mirror-Mambo quickly became popular and many enthusiastic works were made, sometimes with fabrics that would have otherwise probably not found their way into a quilt. I keep finding new and interesting Mambo quilts. Nobody can reinvent the square, but you can certainly have your own interpretation of it. And so I wish you this bit of enthusiasm and fun for making your own creations.

In my second Exercise Book I would like to present some new shapes and patterns that were not in the Exercise Book 1 and also show you some of the wonderful quilts that were made with my templates.

"Whoever keeps a watchful eye upon himself, will not hesitate to hold his tongue when others err."

Johann Wolfgang v. Goethe

Quilting – a few thoughts...

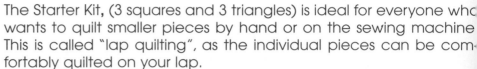

The Starter Kit, (3 squares and 3 triangles) is ideal for everyone who wants to quilt smaller pieces by hand or on the sewing machine. This is called "lap quilting", as the individual pieces can be comfortably quilted on your lap.

The sewing machine industry has had quite a few ideas to make quilting easier for us. The DESIGNER 1 from Husqvarna Viking, for example, incorporates a program setting for free-hand or stipple quilting; when you select it the machine sets itself, lowers the transport foot, and you can start quilting right away. Practise with a simple "sandwich" (top, batting, backing) which has been basted with thread. If you cannot lower the transport foot on your machine cover it with scotch or masking tape. What you will need is a quilting foot and the possibility to set your machine to a darning stitch. Then you can practise free quilting on the machine, designing shapes and even letters. You control the length of the stitches, not the machine. A steady coordination of the up and down movement of the needle and the sideways movement of your quilt guarantees a regular quilting pattern. When you are able to easily write your name in this way, then you will also be ready to quilt shapes and patterns on your quilt: it takes a little practise, like everything in life...

Of course you can also use your quilting foot and sewing machine to quilt straight lines, just try it out.

But for most quilters, hand-quilting remains a cherished hobby, a way of breathing LIFE into their quilt and a moment of quiet meditation to the gentle movements of the needle. And, not to forget, seeing all the beauty you can create with your hands.

"Beauty is a rainbow, a peacock's fan
with its glistening spread of colours.
If a bird can understand this, then I can, too".

Eva Zeisel, honorary doctor Museum of Modern Art,
in response to the question: „What is beauty?"

The different kinds of hand-quilting

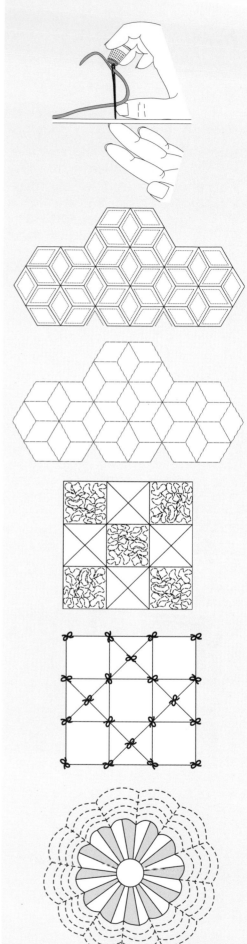

You are probably familiar with different techniques for hand-quilting. Here is an overview of the most well-known ones:

Contour quilting
Quilting the contours of the different pieces of fabric, about 0,6 cm (1/4") from the seam. You can easily mark straight lines with scotch tape or use a pencil or marker that will wash out well.

Quilting in the ditch
Quilting along the seams, this really highlights the different shapes. Another reason this is popular, is because it allows you to hide the quilt stitches a little from close inspection.

Stipple quilting
Meandering quilt lines; a free form is drawn onto a larger area and then quilted by hand or by machine. The area may be determined by the patchwork pieces or set off by a quilted circular border around it.

Tie
The quickest way of finishing your quilt is to tie knots, spaced evenly across the quilt. You prepare the quilt as if you were going to quilt it, that is, basting the three layers together. For the knots, you may use any material you like, such as wool, embroidery thread, quilting thread, laces, whatever you find works best with your quilt.

Echo quilting
The design is outlined by quilt lines at steadily increasing intervals. This technique is often used in Hawaian quilts, to emphasize the different shapes and figures.

Project   Ginie's Starter Kit

With the three squares and the three triangles in Ginie's Starter Kit you will be able to sew countless blocks. The example blocks shown in the drawings should only be the starting-point for your own experiments. And don't limit yourself to 30 cm (12") blocks, expand your creativity to 15 cm (6") or 20 cm (8") blocks.

These instructions explain step by step how you can sew and combine quilt blocks of your choice to make a sampler quilt as shown in the picture. The distinguishing feature of this quilt is that all three layers are sewn row by row. With traditional row-by-row quilts, only the top was produced in this way; afterwards the quilt had to be pinned and quilted like a traditional quilt. That meant you still had to "battle with a monster", either on your sewing machine or in your quilting frame. We spent a long time thinking about how to make machine quilting more attractive, but even as a staunch handquilter you will appreciate the results of this work. Just follow the instructions closely.

A large piece of molton fabric is of great aid here. „Table molton" is a wonderful material, which your fabrics will cling to without pins. You will be able to continually move and rearrange your pattern designs. Attached to your studio wall, it allows you to work with your cut-out pieces with great ease.

A few more words of advice before we begin: all the seams on the top and back of the quilt may be machine-sewn, only the seams for pinning the batting need to be roughly sewn by hand.

Before you start to cut, please mark the templates as shown to the right. In the following instructions the templates will be referred to only by their numbers. Beside each block you will find the required number of shapes. As for chosing your colours, you may take the light and dark shades as a starting point or just let your imagination run freely.

Materials and measurements:

You'll need various scraps to make the blocks (we've used fabric from the JINNY-BEYER-collection) and a solid colour fabric for the sashing and borders (black, in our example). The back of our quilt is simply made up of black, blue and red stripes – what a simple and effective way of combining traditional and modern design! But please feel free to use your own creativity!!

To make a top of 5 x 4 blocks you need:

15 strips of vertical sashing 10 cm (4") x 31.5 cm (12.5")
4 strips of horizontal sashing 10 cm (4") x 180 cm (71") (length somewhat generous)
10 vertical border strips 15 cm (6") x 31.5 cm (12.5")
2 horizontal border strips 15 cm (6") x 180 cm (71") (length somewhat generous)
20 blocks from the block library (starting page 10)
Four blocks plus border/sashing strips make up one row, see also the drawing.

Constructing the Quilt

As this quilt will be completed in rows, you need to decide which block goes where before sewing the blocks together. This will enable you to correctly add the sashing and border strips.

Choose your favorite blocks from our extensive library. If you are designing your own blocks, please keep the following in mind: template 1 can only be used "standing on its point" and templates 3 and 6 in combination with other templates may result in block sizes other than 12"/30 cm – in fact it is quite possible to create blocks of different sizes using these same templates!!!

Assemble your fabrics and prepare everything for cutting.

Use small self-adhesive labels to mark your templates. Do not use permanent markers, as they fade too quickly with handling.

Double Windmill

#3 - 24 x
#6 - 24 x

Rolling Stones

#3 - 20 x
#6 - 32 x

Gretchen

#3 - 8 x
#6 - 56 x

Ocean Waves

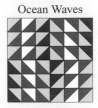

#6 - 72 x

Weatherfane

#3 - 20 x
#6 - 32 x

Broken Dishes

#3 - 20 x
#6 - 32 x

Square of Harmony

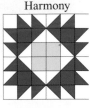

#3 - 12 x
#6 - 48 x

Windowpane

#3 - 4 x
#6 - 64 x

Windmills

#3 - 20 x
#6 - 32 x

Wings of Squares

#3 - 12 x
#6 - 48 x

Box in a Box

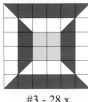

#3 - 28 x
#6 - 16 x

Variable Star

#2 - 8 x
#4 - 4 x
#5 - 8 x

In case your sewing machine doesn't come with a 1/4-inch patchwork foot and you can't adjust the seam allowance manually, you can simply use coloured pencils to mark the sewing lines on your fabric. Nowadays all coloured pencils are lead-free (for the kids), washable, and they won't damage your fabric. And you'll always find a colour that shows up on your fabric!

It is best to arrange the blocks near the sewing machine on a piece of carton, a sheet of sand-paper or a piece of Thermolan (with the last two suggestions the fabric won't slide).

In order to accurately and rapidly cut off the tops of triangles (and avoid so-called "dog-ears") you may also use the "tops-template".

Have you sewn the desired number of blocks and decided which goes where? Then you are ready to add the vertical sashing and border strips to the blocks in order to obtain 5 rows (in our example).

First add the vertical sashing strips between the blocks of the first row.
At the top of your first row of blocks, add the horizontal border strip to the bottom a horizontal sashing strip. Then you need to prepare a backing piece of exactly the same size as your first row plus borders. Your batting needs to be cut 1.5 times the vertical length, that is, when you pin your "quilt-sandwich" the batting needs to go about 8"(20 cm) beyond the edge of the lower sashing strip.

Use cotton batting for machine quilting! It almost sticks by itself to the layers of fabric. Once you have pinned your quilt it is almost guaranteed against slipping: this allows for easy handling of the quilt! For the bobbin thread in your sewing machine we recommend a light cotton thread, such as Cotona 50, in a colour matching your backing fabric. As a top thread also use Cotona 50 or Rayon 40 or smoke-coloured Monofil from MADEIRA (except for completely white tops, where a clear thread works best). Multicoloured and other "special effect" threads also work great. Don't be afraid to try out new things and explore designing with the third dimension through quilting.

Now you have the first complete row, which you can quilt by hand or by machine. Quilt by simply following the seams using "stitch in the ditch" or try other designs like freehand stippling. If your sewing machine includes stitching designs, you might want to experiment with those. The sashing strips in our example were quilted using a design from diskette 101 from HUSQVARNA VIKING on a DESIGNER 1.

Construction in rows (here: 1st row):

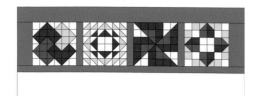

Quilt only the vertical sashing strips and the blocks for now. The complete border will be quilted when the quilt is completely sewn together. The horizontal sashing strip will be quilted once you have added the next row, as you need to keep its bottom edge loose in order to add on the next row by machine.

Assemble your second row of blocks by sewing the vertical sashing strips between the blocks and vertical borders to each side. Then sew one horizontal sashing strip to the bottom of the entire row. Prepare a backing piece of the same size as the entire row.

To add the second row, place the top right sides together, pin and sew. Do the same with the backing pieces. Do not sew through the batting.

The batting overhang from the first row should reach to about the middle of the second row. Prepare a new piece of batting that will reach to about the middle of the third row. Sew the batting pieces together with large stitches. This seam does not need to resist any stress: as it is in the middle of the blocks, the batting will be firmly held in place by the quilting. Again, pin your three layers (top, batting, backing) and quilt the sashing strip from the first row as well as the new row of blocks. Again, leave the horizontal sashing strip unquilted in order to sew on the third row.

Continue in the same way with the other rows: top and backing always need to be of the same size, and the batting reaches halfway into the next row.

In the last row, which ends with the horizontal border strip, you don't need such a long batting overhang.

The advantages of this technique are clear:
When machine quilting you will always work only on the last row of blocks. Yes, on the left side your quilt keeps growing bigger, but on the right side, under the arm of your sewing machine, you will never have a big, bundled-up piece of quilt.

When all the rows and sashing strips have been quilted, you are almost finished! Now you can comfortably quilt around the border and add the binding. Add a label to the back side and maybe a sleeve for hanging (depending on your use of the quilt) and...

...your new masterpiece is ready!

Stripes and Triangles

#5 - 32 x

Five Spots

#3 - 8 x
#6 - 56 x

Judith's Star

#1 - 1 x
#2 - 4 x
#4 - 4 x

Crystal Star

#1 - 1 x
#2 - 4 x
#4 - 4 x
#5 - 12 x

Crossing plate

#4 - 16 x

Colorado Quilt

#4 - 8 x
#5 - 16 x

Dutchman's Puzzle

#4 - 8 x
#5 - 16 x

Brotherly Love

#1 - 1 x
#4 - 12 x
#5 - 4 x

Scrap Basket

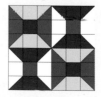

#3 - 7 x
#4 - 4 x
#5 - 10 x

Whirlpool

#1 - 1 x
#4 - 8 x
#5 - 12 x

Spools

#3 - 20 x
#6 - 32 x

Friendship Stars

#3 - 20 x
#6 - 32 x

Sailing boat

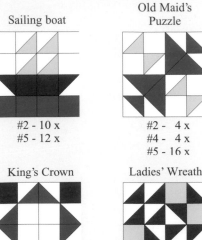

#2 - 10 x
#5 - 12 x

Old Maid's Puzzle

#2 - 4 x
#4 - 4 x
#5 - 16 x

Yankee's Puzzle

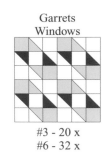

#4 - 4 x
#5 - 24 x

Anna's Favorite

#5 - 32 x

Four T

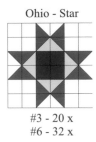

#3 - 12 x
#6 - 48 x

Mosaic Cross

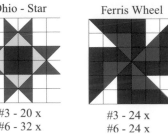

#4 - 6 x
#5 - 20 x

King's Crown

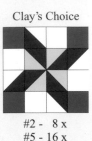

#2 - 8 x
#4 - 4 x
#5 - 8 x

Ladies' Wreath

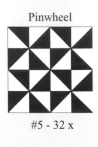

#2 - 4 x
#5 - 24 x

Zig-Zag

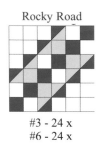

#2 - 12 x
#5 - 8 x

Garrets Windows

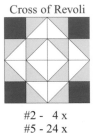

#3 - 20 x
#6 - 32 x

Ohio - Star

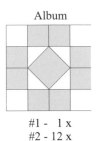

#3 - 20 x
#6 - 32 x

Ferris Wheel

#3 - 24 x
#6 - 24 x

Clay's Choice

#2 - 8 x
#5 - 16 x

Pinwheel

#5 - 32 x

Cross of Revoli

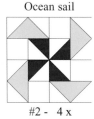

#2 - 4 x
#5 - 24 x

Rocky Road

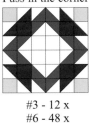

#3 - 24 x
#6 - 24 x

Album

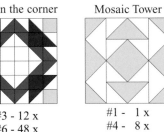

#1 - 1 x
#2 - 12 x
#5 - 4 x

Road to Oklahoma

#2 - 12 x
#5 - 8 x

With the Starter Kit you can do more than just sew blocks as you can see in this example.

Ocean sail

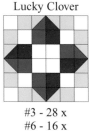

#2 - 4 x
#4 - 4 x
#5 - 16 x

Puss in the corner

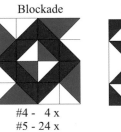

#3 - 12 x
#6 - 48 x

Mosaic Tower

#1 - 1 x
#4 - 8 x
#5 - 12 x

Lucky Clover

#3 - 28 x
#6 - 16 x

Blockade

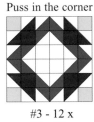

#4 - 4 x
#5 - 24 x

Mosaic Star

#1 - 1 x
#4 - 8 x
#5 - 12 x

Card-trick

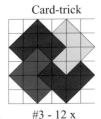

#3 - 12 x
#6 - 48 x

Bow-Tie

#1 - 1 x
#2 - 12 x
#5 - 4 x

Sewn and hand quilted by Bettina Weber

I am often asked how the quilts of "Amish people" are different from others. In response, I like to talk about their history, my visits there, their way of life and the very special hospitality they offered us quilters to make our visits unforgetable experiences.

The food always reminded me of "grandma's recipes" and the large families of times gone by. One gets the feeling that Amish women are capable of anything and that in their lives of simplicity they see a God-ordained destiny.

I firmly believe that everything we do with love has sense and meaning.

Here some pertinent information about the "Amish people" and their quilts from an expert woman on the subject of the Amish, Julie Silber. For decades she acted as curator of ESPRIT's valuable collection, she has presented a great variety of Amish work in various books and remains an undisputed authority.

By the way, the valuable ESPRIT collection "Quilts from Lancaster County" has been bought back by the museum of Lancaster county after a huge fundraising operation collected one million dollars. Starting in 2004, it can again be visited in the museum of Lancaster county.

I organized an exhibition of these extraordinary quilts in my home town of Constance, Germany, and know how carefully they have always been guarded, handled, hung and shipped. Now they will not leave Lancaster again.

But, let's hear from Julie Silber:

Amish Quilts of Lancaster County

Classic Amish quilts – those made between 1860 and about 1950 – may seem incongruous with our image of the Amish people. We can enjoy the quilts on a strictly visual level but, to appreciate them more fully, we should understand something of the culture from which they sprang.

The Amish world began in mid-sixteenth-century Germany when the Anabaptists, a radical Protestant sect, rebelled against the Roman Catholic Church, which they thought had become allied too closely with the war-making state. After generations of horrific prosecution and relocation in Europe, a group of Anabaptists calling themselves Mennonites (for their spiritual leader Menno Simmons) and another splinter Anabaptist group, the Amish (for their leader Jakob Amman) left for the new land of America.

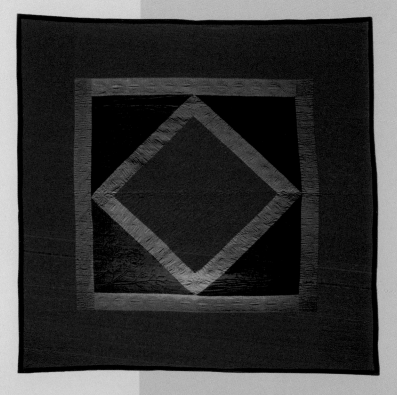

The first small group of Amish immigrants came to Pennsylvania in 1737. Other groups followed in the next two decades and at the beginning of the 19th century. The Amish were part of a larger group of immigrants who came to be referred to as "Pennsylvania Dutch", which included not only the Amish and Mennonite communities but also other Protestant groups from Germany, Switzerland and the Netherlands. Many desired a land of economic opportunity, but the Amish sought freedom of religion above all else.

After fierce prosecution in Europe, the Amish wanted to be able to live their faith and avoid outside influences and progress as much as possible. They set up farm-based communities where they controlled all businesses, educational and spiritual practices. For the most part they succeeded, and today there are over 130,000 Amish in North America, with the largest concentrations in Pennsylvania, Ohio and Indiana.

Fundamental to Amish life is an instruction to be different from the non-Amish, or "English". They carry out that instruction in a variety of ways, from wearing a different kind of clothing to speaking a unique German dialect, from using horse-drawn transportation to avoiding the use of public electricity in their homes. The Amish world follow a construction of practises which perpetuates their status as a people apart, living within the larger American culture. Far from simply continuing to exist, the Amish have actually flourished. Their set of practises and guiding principles is remarkably complete, designed both to perpetuate the Amish way of life and to accomodate change in the external world.

There are two pillars of Amish life, Gemee (or Gemeinde, German for "community") and the Ordnung (German for "rule", "order"). Gemee encompasses the very idea of Amishness, suggesting spiritual community or congregation. It is Gemee that binds the Amish together through submission to the will of God and of the group and Gemee that fosters a powerful desire within the Amish to live apart from the corrupting outside world.

The Ordnung, or "order", gives a practical framework intended to insure the continuance of Gemee. It is a complex set of rules that preserves and strengthens the Amish way of life. It has two parts. The written Ordnung specifies doctrine and creed, spiritual practises and church discipline. It amounts to Amish law and has remained essentially unchanged for hundreds of years. On the other hand, the unwritten Ordnung governs details of everyday life, such as dress, decoration, grooming, use of technology and ways of working. It is not a set of statements to be memorized, but rather a "way of doing things" that is thoroughly and naturally absorbed by all.

The unwritten Ordnung varies considerably among Amish groups. Some groups are allowed buttons on clothing, some only hook and eyes. Some may use white fabric in their quilts, some not. Some are allowed to have telephones at the end of the drive-way for occasional use, some may not have telephones anywhere on the premises.

As quiltmaking entered the Amish life towards the end of the nineteenth century, it was subject to the Ordnung's careful regulation against showiness and freewheeling individuality. Quilters understood that they were to make these bedcoverings from the same fabrics as they used for clothing. They also knew to choose from only a limited number of designs. These designs generally consist of a few, large pieces of fabric, as Amish quiltmakers were likely seeking to avoid the prideful feelings that can come with sewing many small pieces together. Whereas quiltmaking was often exploited by other American women as one of their only viable means of artistic or personal expression, Amish women, who thought of themselves as making blankets, were also expressing the group sensibility. The Amish aesthetic was a reflection of community values.

In a society where the concept of community is foremost, personal innovation may be experienced as threatening to the common good, and it is discouraged. Conformity is highly valued. So, the Amish quiltmakers engaged in making not the showiest or most innovative quilts, but in perfecting traditional designs. Amish quilts, then, tend to harmonize when seen in a group. Of course, no two are exactly alike, as individuals struggle toward the ideal in unique ways.

Aside from using larger fabrics and simpler designs, Amish women made quilts of only solid-colour materials. They employed relatively dense quilting, the stitching that holds the three layers of a quilt together. They used non-contrasting thread, unlike other quilters. While other American quilts come in a bewildering variety of sizes and formats, Amish quilts come in only a few. At a time when other women had hundreds of colours and patterns to choose from, the repertoire of pieced designs and quilting patterns in all Amish communities was small.

One might think that Amish quilts would be all hand-sewn. But Amish quiltmakers are as practical as they are skilled. Treadle sewing machines have been used by Amish quilters since well before the turn of the century. Even the bindings are usually sewn by machine, with clearly visible stitches. Only the masterful, elaborate quilting has always been done by hand.

Among the many Amish communities, differences in quilt styles are fairly easy to see. Midwestern Amish women, for example, commonly used clothing scraps, so that the blocks and even the borders are sometimes made of mismatched pieces sewn frugally together. In Ohio and Indiana Amish quilts, black often predominates. They are typically made of cottons, sometimes cotton sateen.

Holmes County, Ohio, Amish quilters favor repeated, traditional, geometric blocks, in colours ranging from quiet earth tones in earlier ones to combinations of black and various "mint" pastels in later examples. Amish quilts from Indiana use similar blocks and rectangular formats, but with less black and a more liberal use of red. They tend to be less rigorous in design than their Ohio counterparts.

The quilt shown here is from Lancaster County in southeastern Pennsylvania, and is an example of the most distinctive of all Amish

Extra course Amish

During my time spent living in the United States, one of my experiences I would not want to miss were the international luncheons. For mothers it was a good time of day to meet because the American school and kindergarden hours leave plenty of time and working women could take part during their lunch break. There were speeches of all kinds about traditions, custom, folk art and national specialties. If you took part regularly you could get to know almost all about the women's world and get to know a lot of new people. Especially the hosts, the American women, talked about the different aspects of their lives, which I thought of as "fantastically" progressive forty years ago.

I remember particularly well one speech of Pat Kyser. Pat decorated famous halls in Texas and Georgia with her outstanding quilts. Furthermore she is very well known because of her teaching "The Art of Traditional Quilting" at Georgia University. She wanted to preserve an American folk art. She became my first quilt teacher and I want to pass on her basics about quilt making that she taught to hundreds of students. It is still valid today.

How to make a quilt

- I decide on a pattern and pick the fabric.
- I decide on the size of the quilt and calculate the block size. If all fails I have to redraw the original pattern.
- Then I draw the whole quilt on paper. A good scale is 1:8.
- Now I can calculate the required fabric amount and draw plans on how to cut the different colours. I write down how many pieces of each fabric I have to cut.
- Since the fabrics can shrink and/or bleed while washing I prewash and iron before sewing. Following my cutting plan I cut my fabrics beginning with the borders.
- I sew a test block. While ironing I take good care to iron the seam allowances all to one side which should be the darker side. With a ruler I check the measurements. When there are differences I have to adjust the seam allowances. Now I sew all blocks. Working carefully and accurately is a must. Sometimes I have to draw the sewing line on each separate piece. I make sure that all corners fit through ironing, measuring and if necessary correcting. Now I can join the blocks to rows and the rows to a quilt top. Again I have to check that all corners and tips meet accurately. The top is ironed and checked for stable seams and good fit. Sloppiness at this state will not satisfy later on.
- Borders are added with the help of marks at a quarter length and in the middle. The fabric can easily stretch while adding the border. This should be avoided to save folds and pleats in the seam. Iron.

quilts. Lancaster county is home to the oldest continuously occupied Amish settlement in the country. While there are larger clusters of Amish in Ohio and Indiana, this 200-year-old community of Old Order Amish is the most visible, and it has therefore provided the template for many of the popular images of the Amish. It is from the lush farmlands and rolling hills of Lancaster that we have the most familiar pictures of Amish groups in horse-drawn buggies, and of Amish men working fields with teams of horses.

The handful of favored designs in Lancaster probably evolved slowly, in a comprehensible elaboration of the square. The Center Square led to the Diamond in a Square and the Bars. Smaller squares were introduced to make Sunshine and Shadow and Ninepatch quilts. Fairly quiet, restrained crazy quilts, rather scantily embellished in comparison with Victorian crazies, turned up occasionally, as did other American patterns like Irish Chain, interpreted in the characteristic, saturated jewel tones favored by the Amish.

But it was the peculiarities of the Lancaster County unwritten Ordnung that guided Amish women there in making such extraordinary quilts. The restriction against showiness was understood by quilters not as a limitation, but as an invitation to partake of tradition in the same way as their grandmothers, the same way as their granddaughters.

Lancaster County Amish quilters started with a fairly strict, traditional format, not unlike a poet who begins a sonnet. The fabric poem she created would reflect much about the Amish way of life: the wish for simplicity and balance, earthly practicality, a remarkable "centeredness" and focus on community, the individual voice raised only in harmonious praise.

Other reflections of this sensibility, and possible design sources or references, are close at hand: see the simple, clean lines of Amish architecture, the lush colours of their crops laid out within the orderly, well-defined borders of fields, the colourful, organized flower gardens next to the house. Colour is everywhere in Amish life: women wear dresses of royal blue or emerald plum beneath the somber coats and capes we see in town. Children wear especially brightly coloured shirts and blouses. To the Amish, these quilts are as natural as breathing. Take

Diamond in a Square, unknown quilter, Lancaster County, Pennsylvania, circa 1920, wool, pieced

16

out of context and presented on the walls of a museum, these quilts may resemble the "heroic" efforts of highly individualistic twentieth-century painters who followed. In context, however, we can see them as organic expressions of the way of life that produced them, the creations of a culture into which art is thoroughly integrated. Simple, centered, harmoniously colourful and thoroughly well-crafted, Lancaster County Amish quilts place themselves among the finest aesthetic objects ever made. We can study them for their exquisite, graphically sophisticated design and as stunning visual statements, or we can enjoy them for their exquisite craft. We can apprciate them as expressions of a group sensibility – an unspoken agreement between women to make quilts "a certain way". No matter how these quilts are seen, however, they represent a cultural treasure of the highest order.

Information about the Amish: quoted and adapted from an article by Julie Silber
With kind permission from Julie Silber at The Quilt Complex, Albion, CA, USA
Photographs: Courtesey of Julie Silber

- I choose a quilt design and mark it on the quilt top using a pencil that leaves removable lines. The quilt top is ready to be set into a quilt frame. For this you should take your time, because both layering and stretching the separate layers are extremely important. Now it is time to quilt. I make small even stitches and hide the knots between the layers. When the whole quilt is quilted, I take the quilt off the frame. I cut the borders even and bind the quilt with a suitable method.
- Finally the most important: I enjoy my quilt!

Project

The Snowball and its Variations

The easiest way of cutting an octagon (an eight-sided piece) is to mark the diagonals on a square piece and then cut off the corners. Mark the middle distance between the center (the point where the two diagonals cross) and the corner and draw a perpendicular there to cut off the corner. Now you have a perfect octagon (see drawing).

With the octagon in a light colour combined with a dark colour to make a square, we get the first impression of a snowball. In blue and white the pattern is a classic. The snowball pattern has always been a favourite for quilting bees. Each participant contributed a square block with her/his favorite quilting motif in the center. Thus the "snowball-effect" was started and the quilt grew rapidly.

You can prepare your own templates by using the models in the templates' section of the book, or you can buy ready-made Ginie' Templates, which have the additional advantage of incorporating the seam-allowance.

Snowball
On the following pages you will find many ideas and step-by-step instructions for using the snowball sets for 30 cm (12") or 40 cm (16") blocks. This pattern adapts itself well to a small quilt or a greeting card, for example. Bettina has prepared a whole series of examples and here is what I like about them: the imagination in reworking the same theme with different elements. I think I don't have to say much about these examples, they are a great starting point for your own ideas. You will find inspiration, whether you are looking for a gift idea for a cat lover, a horse fan, a Georgia O'Keefe admirer or an apple gourmet. Your present will be remembered.

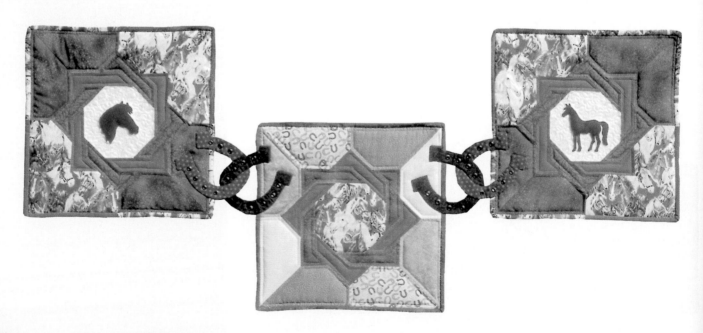

Here are the instructions:
(turn to the template section for the templates)

Each block of the snowball is made up of four elements: the octagon A, the strip B, the triangle C, and the corner pieces D and D reverse (mirror-image).
In total you will need:
1 x octagon A (a print works best)
4 x strip B, light colour
4 x strip B, dark colour
4 x triangle C, light
4 x triangle C, dark
4 x corner piece D
4 x corner piece D reverse (simply flip the template on its back)

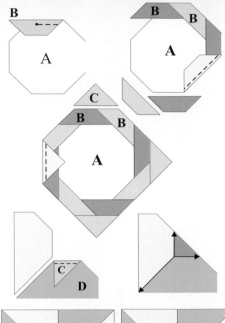

Start with a „partial" seam, that is, don't sew all the way to the end. Sew the octagon right on right to the long side of the strip B. Pin the corner and sew only about 6 cm of the seam, leaving the rest open.
Now continue adding strips going around, alternating light and dark. A part of each B strip is sewn to the octagon, the rest to the B strip preceding it.
Once you have added all the B strips you can close the initial "partial" seam.
Now add the 4 corners (triangle C) – be sure to use the right colours matching the B strips.
Now sew the four borders: to each C piece a D and a D reverse piece need to be added. They are sewn onto the short, diagonal side. Here the (indicated) corner points are very important. Be sure to pin them accurately and not to sew into the seam allowance of the C pieces – the best way is to start your seam at the tip of the C triangles.
Once you have completed the four border strips you can sew them to your block.

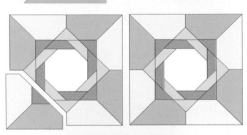

Extra course
Classic Snowball

In this photograph, you can see the octagon designed by Monika Pohl as a "Trip Around the World" in harmonious colours of the sky and the sea. It looks like a very modern design and you almost forget that it is such a traditional pattern. It is a nice challenge to present traditional patterns in a new way so that everybody is surprised at the new look.

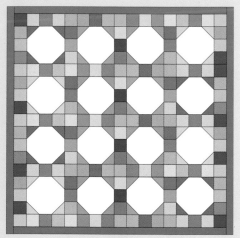

Colour these design sheets with you own favourite colours and come up with new colour combinations. But take a close look: there are three different block variations.

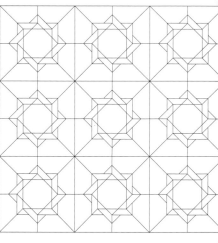

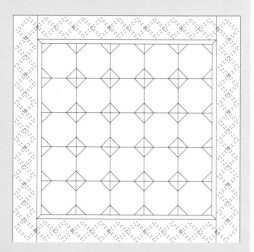

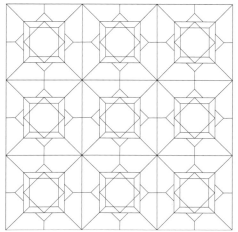

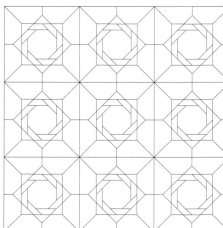

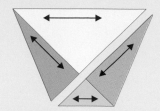

This quilt contains stars made with different template sets. Find out for yourself which templates fit together and create new patterns.

Extra course
Octagon

A star made with templates 54-40 or fight and the octagon.

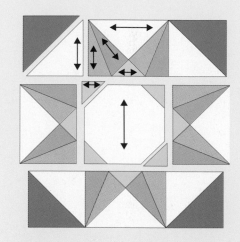

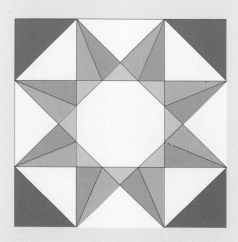

Essay

Fundraiser

to found = 1. To lay the basis of; to set, or place, as on something solid, for support; to ground; to establish upon a basis,
2. To take the first steps or measures in erecting or building up; to furnish the materials for beginning; to begin to raise; to originate

a fund = 1. An aggregation or deposit of resources from which supplies are or may be drawn for carrying on any work, or for maintaining existence.
2. A stock or capital; a sum of money appropriated as the foundation of some commercial or other operation

to raise = 1. To cause to rise; to bring from a lower to a higher place; to lift upward; to elevate
2. To cause to arise, grow up, or come into being or to appear; to give to; to originate

What is behind a „Fundraiser"?

(from Webster's dictionary)

You can easily appreciate the ideas behind this simple word.
In connection with quilting a "fundraiser" has always been a quil that was auctioned off for a good cause or a social event. And many a time, a basis was laid and something was called into being as a result of such a public auction. These valuable quilts certainly contributed large sums of money, maybe for a new school, the roo of a church, a family that was going through hard times, a com munity center, etc. And the lucky people to acquire these work were usually wealthy families that could thus make a public contri bution to the common good. Many of these quilts have been we preserved, as they were stored in expensive chests and now we can admire them in museums and exhibitions. The many, many quilts made for daily use, often lovingly quilted, usually haven' made it to our day and aren't on display in the museums!
Yet it remains a wonderful thing that people think about making a quilt in order to promote a good cause. In the USA you can admire this same spirit in many museums, concert halls, libraries and art col lections, as they are often endowments from millionairs publicly doing their part toward the common good. Just look at the "MET" the MOMA or the Modern Art Museum in Washington, which wa paid for with a cheque from a rich family.

Stars show us the way, give us hope and have an ancient tradition in all cultures.

I saw such need and suffering on my visit to Pakistan that I couldn' just act like nothing happened. The back of the quilt is a hand painted cloth from the community as a thank you for the aid. Thi quilt is being auctioned to provide medicine for the children, as the parents are too poor to pay for them.
Maybe you also know of a special project deserving assistance in your community. Maybe this little chapter about fundraisers ha given you some good ideas…

Did you know that there are 70,000,000,000,000,000,000,000 (70 trillion) stars in the sky shining down at us?
(according to a calculation by Australien astronomers for the known part of the universe)

Here we have a photograh of a very old fundraiser, which was auctioned off for a new school roof and one that should bring in funds for a children's hospital in Multan/Pakistan. Not to wonder that it shows all stars.

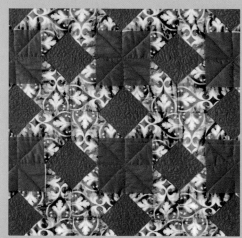

Project

For strip-piecing, set your sewing machine to a shorter stitch. As you are going to cut the strips again with the templates it is best to have strong seams.

To avoid bumps in the finished fabric sew on one strip in one direction, then sew on the next one in the other direction, etc.

I always start the next seam on the side with the long thread from the sewing machine (i.e. turning around the piece).

Arrow, Triangle, Square

With the arrow, triangle and square templates you can make countless patterns. Use the diagram for the tresses to make a scrap quilt, or try working it in a more rustic design, using the scraps from your log cabin strips. These templates also work great to make a Christmas quilt with trees or an Attic Window.

Maybe you like the stars I am presenting here. There are so many variations, especially if you first create your own fabrics by sewing together strips of your favorite material and then using the templates to cut. Put the fabric strips together in ever new combinations and you will have a wonderful variety of "striped" stars. You will have lots of fun making up your own creations.

A few remarks on strip-piecing
(making your own fabric by sewing together strips of other fabrics)

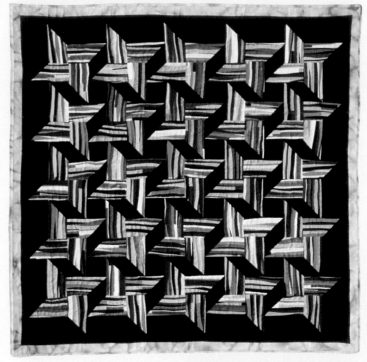

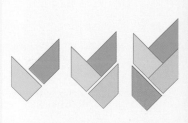

Also try using the mirror technique, as I have done with the border fabrics. They are ideal for the mirror technique. Stack the same design in four layers and pin them together using a long, flat pin. You can do the same with any other kind of fabric. You just need to keep in rapport to the number of repeating pieces. (see border star quilt, page 23)

Essay
St. Koloman

It was around the year 1000, when a young prince decided to leave the palace and learn about the world. Maybe he enjoyed travelling incognito and didn't want to be laughed at while on his search for God and love. The people of Stockerau took him to be a spy and decided that he should die by hanging.

They must have revelled in their feeling of justice, while taking the descision to rub out a young life in order to avoid any upset to their daily affairs.

It was to be done quickly and set a deterring example for the community. These were the rough ways of people who had rough lives, working hard to earn their daily bread.

But the on-looking crowd was to witness a miracle on that day. The legs of the young man had barely stopped moving when the eyes of the men and women watching turned to the elder tree: it started budding and then forming flowers of radiating colour.

Now everyone knew that the hanged man had been a Saint, and the news spread faster than any other.

Even today people in Austria pray to Saint Koloman when they are in great need, and many miraculous events are attributed to his help.

When on your way to Vienna, stop to visit the magnificent monastery of Melk and its valuable treasures. And be sure to

Elder flower quilt –
delicious juice and a remarkable legend

When I look at this quilt, I think of elder flowers. Barbara told me about her experiences when going out early in the morning to harvest the flowers with the morning dew. She prepares a juice with them that makes a delicious cocktail with champagne or sparkling wine (see recipe).

Elder berries also remind me of the legend of St Koloman, who is revered as the patron saint of the Austrian town Melk.

Elder flowers by Barbara Malanowski-Casty

The elder bush is a very special plant. It is in flower from the end c May until the beginning of July. Its small, white and yellow flower forming clusters that are called umbels.

In late summer, it bears shiny berries of a dark violet hue.

The priest and natural healer Sebastian Kneipp (1821-1897) wrote „there shouldn't be a house that doesn't have an elderbush close by".

In the natural religion of the old Germanic tribes, the crown of the elder bush was the home of the goddess Holda or Holla, protecte of home and hearth. (In old German crown=tar, holluntar, ancesto of the modern German Hollunder, the elderbush.)

In the fairy tales of the Grimm brothers we find her as "Frau Holle" shaking out and making up the beds in the morning. Here she is the symbol of a hard-working, housekeeping, open-hearted and wise woman.

There is an old saying „Vorm Holunder, den Hut herunter" (Take off your hat, when before an elderbush).

A typical property of the elderbush is its rapid growth and its incredible regenerating power.

It is sung in children's rhymes because it protects the house it grows in front of!

People believed that the energy for the rapid growth exhausted any evil energy in the vicinity and so could help an ill person recover.

The dark red juice of the berries was used to dye fabrics.

From the elder flowers you can prepare a delicious syrup. A flower sherbet or a cocktail of flower syrup and light, Italian champagne (Prosecco) will be a wonderful addition to your next garden party!

look at the golden monstrance of Saint Koloman decorated with elder leaves and flower petals richly decorated with precious pearls in memory of the young prince and Saint.

ELDER
"Holunder wirkt Wunder"
("elder works miracles", German rhyme)

ELDER FLOWER JUICE

Ingredients:
3 umbels (clusters) of elder flowers
500 g sugar
1 big lemon
125 g wine vinegar (5%)

Preparation:
1. Place the flowers – which should be harvested in the early morning hours to have the richest flavor – in a stone or earthenware jug and cover with 3 liters of boiling water.
2. In a bowl dissolve the sugar in another 3 liters of water and add the sliced lemon and the vinegar.
3. Let sit for 1 hour, stirring occasionally. Then add to the stone jug and mix well.
4. Close the stone jug and leave it in a warm place for 3 days.
5. Then fill the juice into bottles, cork them well, and let sit another 12–15 days until the "wine" is ready for drinking.

A German children's rhyme:
„Ringel, Ringel, Reihe
sind der Kinder dreie,
sitzen unterm Hollerbusch,
schreien alle: husch, husch, husch !"
tells of three children sitting
under an elderbush.

Elder berry juice is a wonderful flu medication:
Heat 1/2 l elder berry juice with 1/4 l black tea, 2 cloves, a little lemon zest and a stick of cinnamon. Sweeten with two tablespoons sugar or honey. ("take your hat off in front of the elder"), as its flowers bring good luck to its owners!

Elder, black pearls
among the fruits of nature

Elder contains many valuable ingredients such as essential oils, organic acids, the minerals potassium, phosphorous and magnesium, as well as pro-vitamin A, vitamins of the ß group and vitamin C.

Project

Dresden Plate

This is a traditional appliqué pattern, which was most likely taken along to the New World from porcelain painting in Dresden.

This pattern has been described in detail in my Exercise Book 1. Should you ever visit the Semper Opera in Dresden, be sure to look up at the ceiling, where you will find the original design (in my opinion).

I have created a block with this well-known and popular pattern. With the templates you can easily sew 30 cm (12") or 40 cm (16") blocks, as shown in the drawings. Just study the ideas and drawings and find your own colour combinations, you will see how much fun it is!

For each block you need:
12 center pieces B
4 outer pieces C
4 outer pieces D
4 outer pieces D reverse
1 center circle A

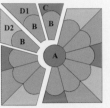
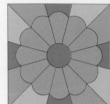

Begin with the curved seams: the four outer pieces C are sewn on to four center pieces B. Do the same with outer pieces D and D reverse. Sew three of the thus obtained pieces together along the now straight edges to form a quarter block.

Sew two quarters together to obtain half a block and then attach the center circle. You may also appliqué the center circle onto the finished block.

28

Experiment with prints: a repeating pattern is arranged in a circle using the Mambo technique to achieve stunning results.

Extra course
Dresden Plate – oval

Here is a different idea for this pattern: the oval Dresden Plate. You will find templates for it at the end of the book. Apply the center piece last with this version. Another variation is the almost rectangular Dresden Plate. The templates for it are labelled "Dresden Plate 40 cm Exkurs". Here, too, it is best to apply the center piece last.

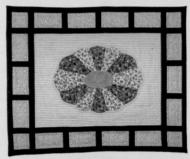

29

Wedding Ring

The Wedding ring is made up of four differently shaped pieces Using the templates you can cut out the pieces and mark the seam lines.

melon

ring

center piece

square

When you have decided how many rings your quilt should have you can easily count the number of different pieces to cut ou using the diagrams. As for colours, the ring and square pieces go together – they make up the wedding rings in the quilt – and the melon and center pieces make up the background. Of course, you can also develop your own variations of the colour scheme.

The center piece is cut from a folded piece of fabric. Place the straight edge of the template (without seam allowance) on the fold in the fabric. Cut out and unfold. And don't forget to mark the seam lines on the whole piece.

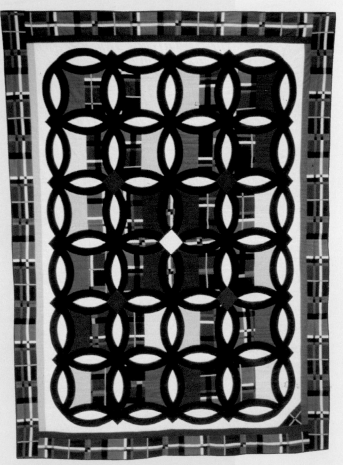

If you don't have much experience with curved seams you should make a few samples before plan ning and cutting a big quilt-top. You will quickly grow to like the wedding ring.
Begin by cutting and laying out your entire design It is easiest at this stage to make a few modification and mark all your pieces.
Mark the middle of the melon and ring piece along the edge with a little cut in the fabric. Then put a ring and a melon piece right sides togethe with the ring on top. You can pin the seam line together to help you with the sewing of the curved seam.

Sew the ring and melon pieces right sides togethe unfold and iron the seam allowances.

Then add the two squares to the opposite ring piece. Iron the seam allowances toward the ring piece.

Now you can sew the two pieces together along the long, curved line. You should end up with a melon-shaped piece.

When sewing curved seams make sure that the center and corner points match exactly. When opened and ironed your piece should lie flat, without bumps or folds at the seam. It is important to sew accurately here, so that your pieces fit together well later.

Now sew the obtained melon-shaped piece to a center piece. Begin at one corner of the seam line and be sure not to go beyond the opposite corner. Secure both ends of the seam with backstitching.

To one center piece, you will add four melon-shaped pieces, one after the other.

Depending on the size of your quilt, you will also need a certain number of center pieces with just two or three melon-shaped pieces added to them to go into the corners and on the sides. Use center pieces to connect completed rings. You get the best overview when laying out the entire quilt after cutting all the pieces. Here is an example design using 12 rings.

First sew together these pieces, then sew the rows together from left to right. Finally, the rows are sewn together along the long seam lines to form the completed quilt top.

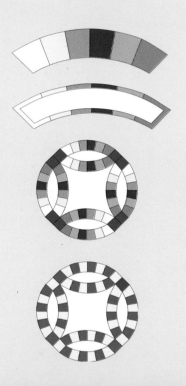

Traditional wedding ring

Traditionally the wedding ring is made up of many scraps, which in turn make up the rings. Using the templates in the appendix you can cut out these pieces in gradations going from light to dark or vice versa from leftover strips and scraps. After sewing together six of these pieces you can use the ring template to correct the curves.

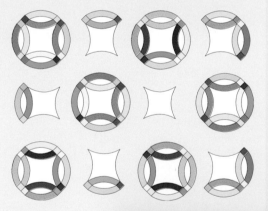

Normally a wedding ring quilt stays rounded at the edges. With my new templates, you can easily fill out the rings to have straight edges and corners.

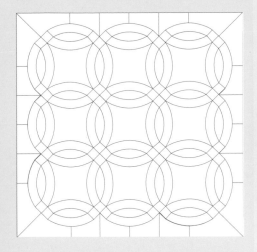

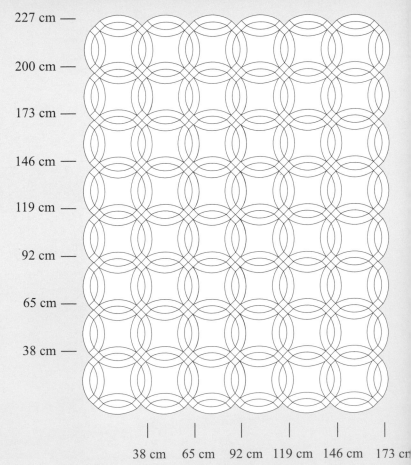

227 cm —

200 cm —

173 cm —

146 cm —

119 cm —

92 cm —

65 cm —

38 cm —

38 cm   65 cm   92 cm   119 cm   146 cm   173 cm

Feng Shui

Feng Shui is the ancient Chinese art of harmony and placement. It is based on laws of balance – we might say moderation – and on the premise of a free-flowing Chi = energy, the basis for health and happiness. Feng Shui teaches that the Chi must flow harmoniously in order to achieve happiness, wealth and a long life.

Feng Shui is also the idea that all life consists of five basic elements: earth, wood, water, metal and fire (the Chinese divide the world into five elements, compared to our classical four).

There are always trends coming from the mysterious Far East, and often they are hardly new; but maybe we like rediscovering old truths in a new light. After all, any modern book on "wellness" will inform you that pleasure in moderation is positive and that our life energy can be increased by positive thinking.

The Chinese started building according to Feng Shui rules as long as 3000 years ago. All the complex little rules of Feng Shui are difficult to grasp for us Europeans, as we are not at all familiar with its comprehensive system of energy flows and elements.

The probably most famous Feng Shui house stands on Hongkong's Repulse Bay. The architects left a giant hole in this huge apartment block, so that the dragon spirit that lives on the hill behind the house may have a clear view of the water of the bay!

So what may be the connection between Feng Shui and quilting? Well, I think a good quilt has a lot to do with harmony, placement, energy and colours. All of these make up a quilt!

So why not try and use the colours that Feng Shui associates with the elements and different aspects of life to make a quilt? Then you can be sure that while you are under its cover, positive energy will flow freely through out your sleep. What a nice wish that is when giving it as a present!

earth
yellow, brown, orange
autumn
complete unity,
shelter, peace

wood
green
spring
family, good health
life, growth

water
black, purple, all emotion
career, strength and knowledge

metal
white, gold, silver
children, leadership

fire
red,
south, summer
health, passion
maximum energy

Do you know how much positive energy you can build up by singing a song that inspires you or speaks to your heart?

Did you know that language labs use the Piano Concerto Nr. 21 by W. A. Mozart to increase concentration while learning?

You can only be creative when you think positive.

Essay

Project
54-40 or Fight

The names of patchwork patterns often have a relation to American history. So, for example, with the pattern "54-40 or fight".

The 54-40 refers to a geographical degree of latitude (which today represents the border between Alaska and north-western Canada):

In the year 1818, the still young United States, together with the British empire and its crown colony British Canada, undertook the joint government of the vast territory to the west of the Rocky mountains, between 42° and 54°40' of latitude, named the "Oregon territory". After fifteen years of joint government, it was decided to divide up this territory between the two countries.

In the American elections of 1844, the democratic candidate, James K. Polk, coined the famous slogan "54-40 or fight", claiming the entire Oregon territory on behalf of the United States. He won the elections and two years later reached a compromise with England that seperated the territory along the 49th degree of latitude, todays border between the USA and Canada.

What remains is history, and another patchwork pattern with a surprising title.

The name of the pattern has historical roots, but its interpretation in pastel colours and flower prints reminds more of summer, energy and happiness. The combination with the log cabin pattern is traditional. Copy the drawings of this pattern and design your own colour scheme for 54-40 or fight! Let your own imagination play with it and explore its manifold possibilities.

Variations by Bettina Weber

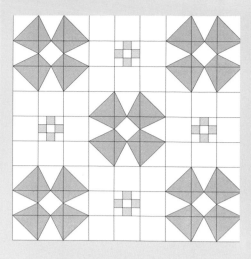

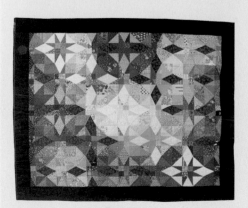

Pat Kyser

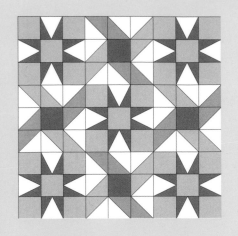

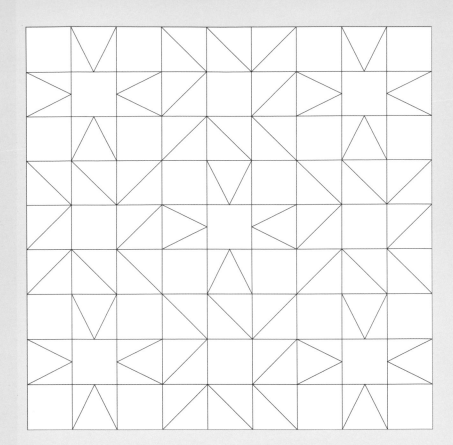

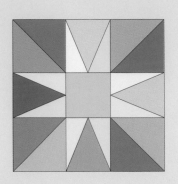

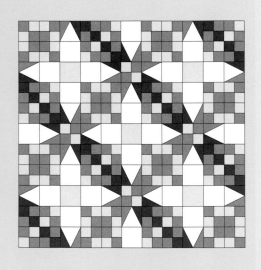

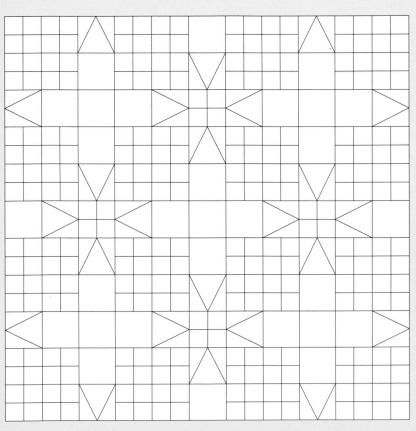

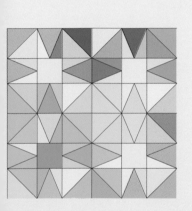

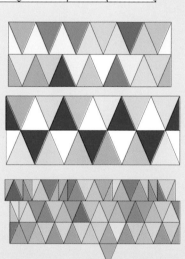

Scrap quilt made by Eli Thomae

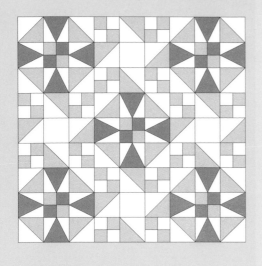

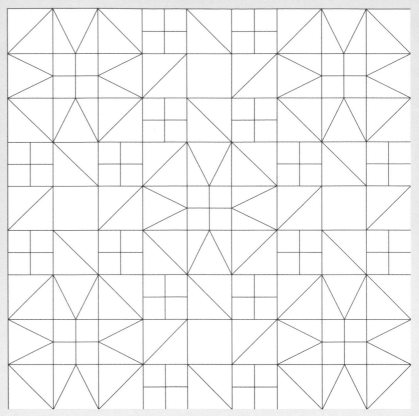

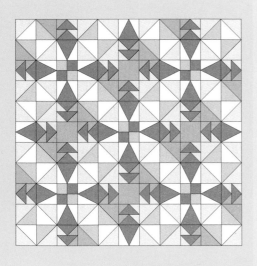

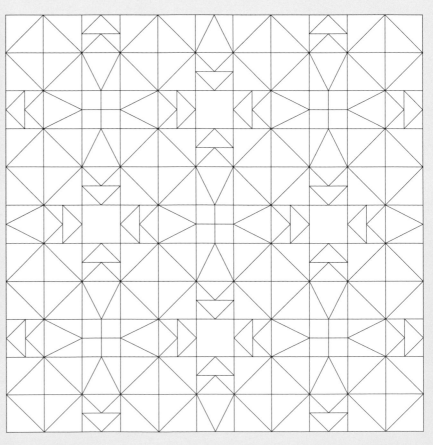

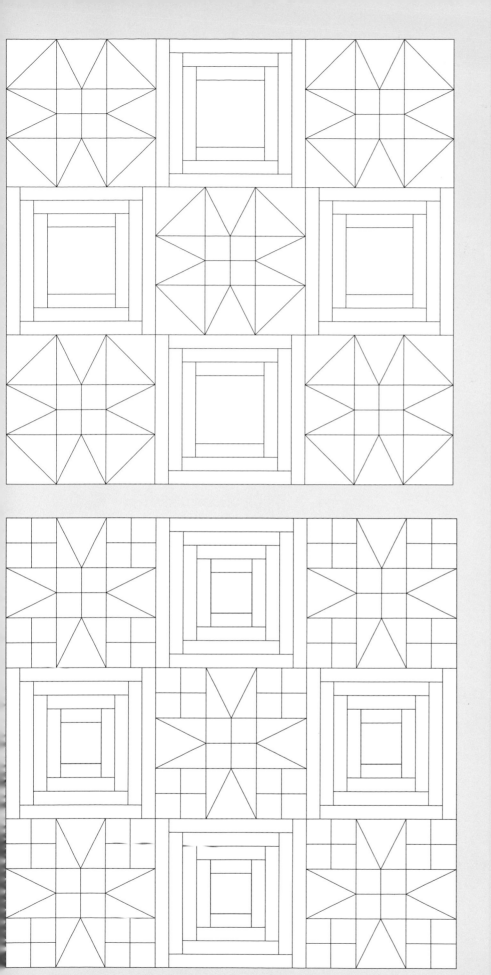

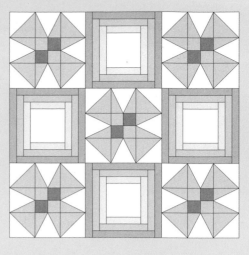

Project

Tennessee Waltz

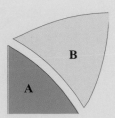

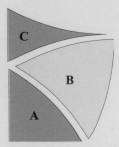

This pattern has an immense variety that animates us to play. Use the diagram and try out your own colour creations.

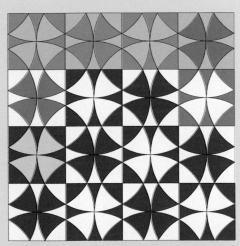

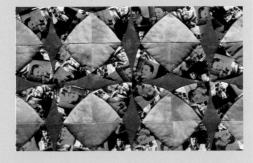

40

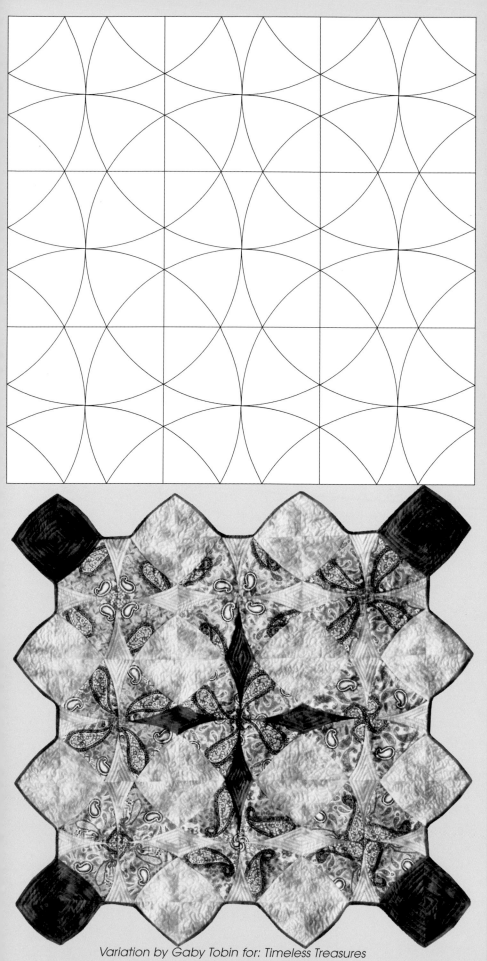

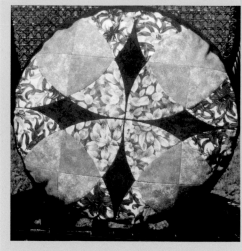

Variation by Gaby Tobin for: Timeless Treasures

Project

Atarashii Patchwork

The Japanese folding techniques, also known as Origami o[r] Atarashii patchwork, are an inspiration for your own creativity. From a multitude of individual patchwork "pockets", which can easily be sewn while travelling, a fascinating two-sided quilt is made piece by piece – an invitation for your own experimentation.

Use the large circular template to cut a circle from the fabric[;] place the template on the fabric and cut along its edge with [a] small rotary cutter. Or mark the circle on the left side of the fabric[,]

with a pencil and the[n] cut it out with scissors. I[f] you want to patch you[r] circle, use the quarter cir[-] cle template. Simply cu[t] out the pieces along it[s] edges (the seam allowances are included) and sew the circle[s] together. Then continue with either step 2a or 2b.

2a) Using the square template, cut out a square of fabric and one of batting. The circle will become the back side and the four rounded edge pieces the top, and the square will appear as the center (yellow) of the pattern.

Iron the seam allowance over the edges of the smalle[r] circle template. You don't need to pin it. Continue with step 3.

2b) Cut out a second circle, including seam allowance. Place the two circles right sides together and sew, using the foot of your sewing machine as a guide along the edge to keep a constant seam allowance.
Attach a square of batting using a strip of Steam-A-Seam and iron (it sticks without ironing, too). Fixing the batting this way keeps it from moving.
Carefully make a cut in the fabric along one edge of the batting and turn everything inside out. Iron the circle again and continue with step 3.

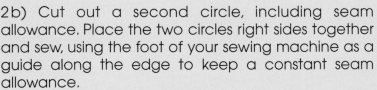

3. Now use the square template to iron over the four edges of the circle. If you are working according to 2a, you now need to place a batting and a fabric square inside the "pocket" of fabric. Pin the round, folded

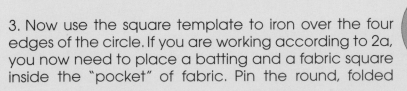

edges to the center over the square fabric using Steam-A-Seam or flat pins and quilt along the curved edges.

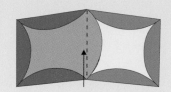

Before sewing the individual pieces together, lay out and arrange your whole quilt. Remember that each piece has a front and back side. Then your finished quilt will look great on both sides!

The individual pieces are now sewn together along the edges, using an invisible or a mattress stitch. Or select a decorative stitch on the sewing machine to sew together.

As an alternative you could also join the squares with a straight stitch before quilting the curves, first joining squares to rows, then joining the rows to make the finished quilt.

Patchwork design using quarter circles

The quarter circle template allows you to make a great variety of different designs. Easily change ideas for the front or back of your quilt. And by giving a little twist, you can double your possibilities!

Example 1: Patch the circles using the quarter circle template. For the inside squares it is best to use a strong contrast colour. When sewing the pieces together, use them right side up and upside down alternatingly.

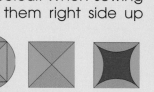
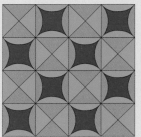

Example 2: Divide your fabrics into two groups, light and dark, for example, or blue and beige, and cut into quarter circles. Now assemble the circles so that they seem to be made up of two halves. Cut the center squares alternatingly from each of the two groups.

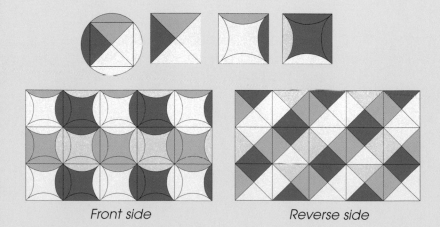

Front side   *Reverse side*

Example 3: This design was worked according to the instructions in 2b: two circles made up of quarter circles are placed right sides together and sewn together along the edge. As described in 2b, the batting is added, the piece turned inside out and then ironed over the square template and quilted.

Further variations on the pattern

...using strip-piecing

You can achieve wonderful results using fabrics you have assembeled yourself beforehand using long strips of fabric. It doesn't matter whether you work very precisely or a little "crazy", you will love the new possibilities and variety!

Example 1: Cut strips of the same width and assemble them so that there is a clear division of colours in the middle (in our example blue on the left and beige on the right). When folded, the divide runs diagonally across the square.

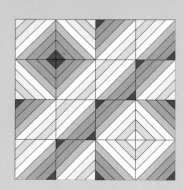

Example 2: achieve great effects with irregular stripes juxtaposed with solid colours. Our advice: don't cut the strips too thin because of the seam allowances (3 cm = 1 1/4" minimum width).

    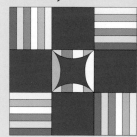

...with "Tie" or "Bow-tie"

Traditional patterns, too, can be assembled and refined with the Japanese folding technique. The "Tie" and "Bow-tie" patterns are hardly recognizable here...

Example 3: Simply cut the finished Bow-tie block into a circle. Iron the seam allowance and fold over a square. Depending on how you orient the square in relation to the circle you can achieve different results.

Example 4: The Tie pattern already is an invitation to experiment. No two designs are the same. In our example the ties are made up of different shades of blue. The solid orange center square was also replaced by ties. The randomly placed yellow accents add life to this playful design.

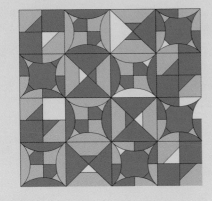

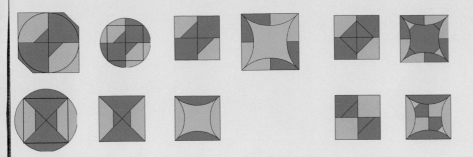

...with curves

Even patterns with curved lines can be given a new twist with the folding technique. Don't be put off by the complicated look: these designs are much easier to make than they appear.

Example 5: The double twist – iron the curves of "Peter and Paul" over the square.

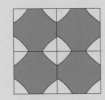 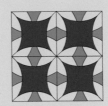

Example 6: Add further circle pieces to "Peter and Paul" – and you will get an additional colour corner.

Example 7: With the "Rounded Triangles" you obtain a dynamic block, almost a windmill. In the drawings you can see how a slight change in the colour scheme will yield a completely different design.

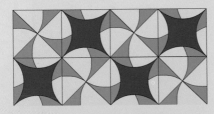

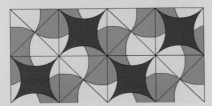

Essay
Blooming Meadow

Rumanian meadows in flower
by Eli Thomae

In the year 2001 I made a trip through Rumania, an impressive country. As a quilter two particular impressions remained in my memory:
the multitude of ornaments
the flowery meadows

The different waves of immigration sweeping through the country in the last centuries have created a great variety of culture and religion, which manifests itself in the different styles of churches and decorations. I drew sketches and made photos of hundreds of mosaics and ornaments. The little notebook I always carry in my purse is full of them.

Another striking aspect of this country is the technologically underdeveloped countryside and agriculture. I felt transported back to the time of my grandparents when I saw a little Panje-wagon, drawn by two horses, bringing home the hay harvest. Of course it looks very romantic at first sight, but it also requires a lot of hard, physical labour. A side effect of this poor and simple farming, however, are the beautiful meadows with

Project Blooming Meadow

I really enjoyed the flowery meadows from the Eli Thomae textile studio, especially, as you can imagine, the playful use of different templates such as triangles, kaleidoscope, equilateral triangles, kite, hexagons and squares. You will surely agree that sewing together these flowers is a special pleasure. Just follow the drawings, it's easy. The photos of Eli Thomae's quilts will make you want to try it out and help you with your first colour selections. Read Eli's story.

When making the blocks, it is important that all the angles around the center add up to 360°. For this reason it is best to work with templates, it avoids any difficult calculations. In order to individually design the petals, I cut them full size using the templates and then sew on the center and add the green outside pieces using the folding technique (see drawing). To make sticking to the colour scheme easier, I number the centers of the petals with chalk.

Cut the individual pieces again using the templates, then the flowers can be easily assembled. (You may have to fill up the outsides.)

Once you start experimenting you will quickly come to realize just how many flowers are hiding inside your templates

their unique variety of wild flowers and colours and heady perfume. Of these I also made many sketches and annoyed my fellow travellers with promises of making a quilt out of them. My plan was delayed for health reasons, but the beginning of the year found me preparing a class called "spring awakening" and I remembered my Rumanian sketches. After a brief look at them, I realized that the same flower shapes appeared again and again, pieces fitting into each other like patchwork. Most of the flowers have a center and a different number of petals; these are block structures known from traditional patchwork: kaleidoscope, four patch, nine patch, triangles, diamonds...

Project

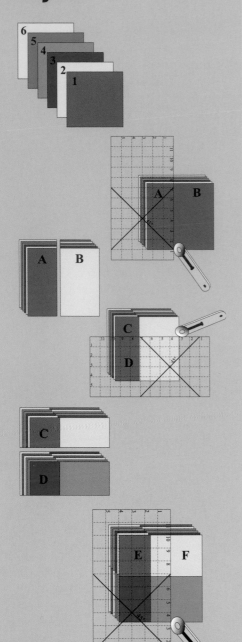

For beginners

This well-known technique is a favorite with patchwork teachers a an introductory exercise to the free work with textiles.

Prepare six 40 x 40 cm squares (16 x 16") of fabric. Use little sticker to number them in order.
Stack them accurately and make a cut through them using a rule and rotary cutter to obtain two stacks. In stack B take the top piece and put it on the bottom of the stack. Then sew the newly obtained halves together, iron and stack them in the original order.
Be sure to keep your pieces in the same order!
You can iron the seam allowances open or toward the darker fab ric, as you prefer.
Again cut through the stack using ruler and rotary cutter to obtain two stacks C and D. In stack D place the top two pieces at the bot tom of the stack.
Again, carefully sew the pieces together in the correct order, iron them and stack them. Make a third cut to obtain stacks E and I place the top three pieces of stack F at the bottom of the stack Carefully sew the pieces together, iron and restack. If you stuck to the correct order, each piece should now be composed of six dif ferent fabrics.
After the fourth cut you place the top 4 pieces at the bottom c one stack, after the fifth cut the top 5, etc. I recommend a maxi mum of 4 to 6 cuts, otherwise the pieces will become too thick fo cutting or too small.
Now measure your pieces. Using the smallest piece as a reference cut them into squares of equal size.
To make a bed-cover you need between 12 and 36 squares pro duced in this way. Lay out your squares, then sew them together ir rows, and finally sew the rows together to form the quilt top. Add borders if you like. Prepare a backing fabric and put together the quilt sandwich (top, batting, back). Quilt by hand or by machine add binding around the edge and you have a wonderful, very per sonal work.

Back of Barbara Malanowski-Casty's quilt using free hand cutting

Advanced projects

This method takes some concentration, but it opens up endless new possibilities. You can also use it to create interesting backgrounds, borders, etc.
The difference to the above method is that all the cuts are made at once, and that diagonal and partial cuts are included as variations.

Stack six 40 x 40cm (16 x 16") squares.

After making the desired cuts, rotate the pieces in the stacks as in the beginners' technique, without losing track of the order.

Be sure to maintain the correct order!

Sew the pieces back together in each layer with care. Iron.
Measure your pieces and use the smallest as a reference to cut six equal squares.

You can make a complete quilt as described in the beginners' technique.

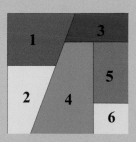

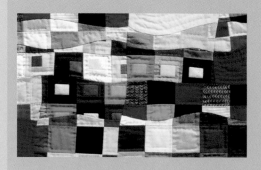

Problems / advice

When making diagonal cuts, don't worry if pieces don't align exactly around the edges. Some width gets lost in the seam allowance.

The same is true for partial cuts.
Always sew from an existing seam or from the center – the edges will be cut straight at the end.

Wave cut

The Wave cut is another interesting method of creating fabric variations.

Stack four pieces of fabric.
Use a rotary cutter to cut wave-like strips.
Rotate the pieces in the stacks as described in the cutting technique above.
Carefully sew the strips together using a narrow seam allowance and not stretching the fabric.
Just as carefully iron the seam allowances to one side.

You can add another wave cut vertically. There are no limits to trying out your own ideas.

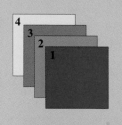

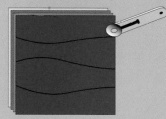

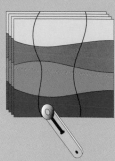

51

Carpet Cut

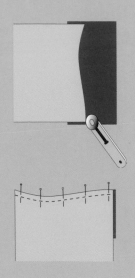

This cut is used to join two irregular edges of fabric.

Place the edge that serves as cutting line so that it overlaps the edge of the other fabric. Both fabrics are right side up. Now use the rotary cutter to carefully cut along the edge of the top fabric. Keep the curves gentle.

Place the two pieces rights sides together and sew with care. Pin the edges to facilitate sewing. Be sure to use a narrow seam allowance (4–6 mm, <1/4") to keep the fabric from stretching.

Here, too, it is best to iron the seam allowances to one side.
Use the carpet cut as often as you like; again, there are no limits to your imagination.

Free-hand cutting

Stack two pieces of fabric right side up and make a free-hand cut with the rotary cutter. Invert the pieces in one of the stacks and sew the different halves together using a narrow seam allowance.

Iron the seam allowances to one side.

Use narrow seam allowances. (5-6 mm maximum)
Pin curved seams before sewing.
Avoid stretching the fabric !

Curves: keep them gentle, not too sharp!

Welcome to the soup kitchen; vegetable soups are a great source of vitamins and health – if you feel like doing something good for yourself, prepare a delicious soup for yourself and your family.

recipe for a vegetable soup:

carrots, celery and leak	clean and dice, you need about 600 gr
3–4 potatoes	Peel and cut the potatoes into small pieces (about 400 to 600 gr). On a small flame, fry the washed and diced vegetables in the butter. Then cover them with boullion and cook until tender.
20 gr butter	Puree the cooked vegetables with a blender. Then add hot boullion until you reach the desired thickness.
ca. 1,5 l Bouillon salt, nutmeg	Salt carefully, add a little freshly grated nutmeg, serve in hot bowls and accompany with fresh bread.

You can vary this recipe in many ways. For example, use just one kind of vegetable, for example fennel, cauliflower, carrots, broccoli etc. This allows you to always make great soup using fresh, seasonal produce.

Mirror-Mambo
Mirror – Stack – Cut – Adore

Discover the endless possibilities of using printed fabric. The Mirror-Mambo method is a valuable addition to variety in patchwork. You can use this method with all of my templates, be they triangles, Kite, Kaleidoscope or any other basic geometric shape.

A few basics:
Be aware of the direction of the weave of the fabric as you cut.
Spray-starch or other ironing aides facilitate the sewing of biased edges (edges cut diagonally across the weave of the fabric).
Seam allowances are included in the templates. So you will lose a little bit at the edges.
Be sure to follow these step-by-step instructions.
If you are working with shapes or sizes that don't correspond to the templates use a patchwork ruler. 60° and 45° angles are usually marked on them, so they are easy to use for cutting your pieces.

Use large, colourful prints with different designs, e.g. flowers, animals or colourful ornaments.
You need as many "rapports" (copies of the image in the mirror) as your pattern contains pieces: for a hexagon, for example, you would need six rapports.
When looking at the design in the folding mirror the apex represents the center, the bottom edges of the mirror are on the future seam lines. If you open the mirror at a 90° angle, you will get a design made up of four pieces, at a 60° angle six pieces, and at a 45° angle eight pieces.

1. Mirror

Place the mirror at the desired angle – 60° in our example – on the fabric. The easiest way to get the correct angle is to align the mirror with your template.

In the mirror you will see how the design develops around the apex (center). Try placing the mirror on different points on your fabric, until you find your favorite.

Be aware of the weave of the fabric. It is preferable to have at least one unbiased edge.

2. Stack

When you have decided on your design, you need to stack your fabrics. Remember, you need as many layers as there are pieces in your pattern, so, six for our hexagon.

Study your print. You will see that the design repeats in regular intervals.

Use some distictive feature – a flower, the eye of a fish or a butterfly – to place six equal strips of fabric on top of each other and pin using Japanese flat pins. This way you make sure that you get an accurate design.

3. Cut

Cut the six strips to the width of the template. Place the template on the fabric and cut along its edges with a rotary cutter. This way you get six hexagons with one cutting.

Look at the weave of the fabric and use flat pins to mark the edge that is parallel to it: the opposite tip will become the center of the hexagon.

Now the diamonds are cut in two at the center. You will have two sets of equilateral triangles.

Have you decided on a background fabric? A solid works best here, whether dark, white or in a bright colour is entirely up to your taste. Again use the diamond template to cut out equilateral triangles. You will need these to join the hexagons to rows.

4. Sew

Use the six identical triangles to make the hexagon. First, sew two triangles together, then add a third. Two such pieces are sewn together to form the hexagon.

Use the solid background triangles to join the hexagons to rows, and finally sew the rows together to finish your patchwork creation. Be sure to always use a constant seam allowance, the width of your sewing foot for example.

55

Mirror-Mambo

           ...with the kite

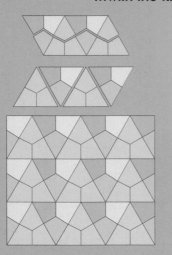

Mirror-Mambo

           ...with the 45°diamond

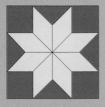

Mirror-Mambo

           ...with the kaleidoscope

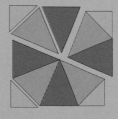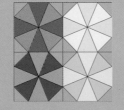

Mirror-Mambo

           ... with the Windmill

5. Adore

So easy – and yet surprisingly new and full of possibilities! Try out different fabrics and different patterns. You will see how exciting these designs can be.

If you want to use the entire diamond instead of cutting it into equilateral triangles as described in step 3 above, try the following:
Cut out diamonds from the background fabric and then lay out the complete design. For sewing, organize three diamonds to make one piece (do you recognize the Baby Blocks?), then use these pieces to build up rows and finally the complete top.

Meeting with Native American Women

Meeting with Hopi-, Navajo, Apache- and Yawapai-tribe quilters

I have had the pleasure of meeting exceptional women from all over Europe, America, Russia, Canada, Australia, Pakistan, Sri Lanka, India, Africa, New Zealand, etc., who have discovered quilting as their hobby and created wonderful quilts, With these works of needle and thread, women and sometimes men, around the globe express what they feel in their souls.

In order to prepare myself for meeting with these Native American women from different tribes, I tried to read as much as I could about their customs and their history. Try it for yourself! It is a fascinating history that brings you in close touch with nature. I studied the books by Dr. Joyce Mori about the patterns used in Native American basket weaving and pottery. In one of her latest books, she has collected them as quilt designs, explaining where each pattern came from, be it from a woven Sioux carpet, a painted vase from the Navajo, or one of the beautiful basket weaves of the Hopi.

A quilt exposition in the Indian Culture Museum in Santa Fé, New Mexico, had me admiring the extraordinary quilts made by Native American women. Organizing a meeting between these women and my German and Swiss quilt groups became part of the dreams I wanted to make come true. It is easy to explain why: because behind each work is not only the environment, and the cultural history of its creator, but also the destiny of individual women, which I enjoy discovering. Also I am fascinated by the craftsmanship and the use of colours which capture our interest.

The meeting was to take place in a hotel in Flagstaff, where we would spend a couple of days together. There was a long and friendly exchange of letters to set it all up. The main part of the meeting would be the "show and tell", showing and explaining our works to each other. I hoped that describing the ideas and motives behind all our works would bring us closer together!

On a beautiful day, we met together at the Hopi Learning Center and learned about what a matriarchal culture means in day-to-day life: the woman chooses her husband, the house and the children belong to her. The mothers-in-law decide whether or not the wedding can take place. The man weaves the bridal gown from black and white wool, incorporating the symbols of life. It is nature that provides for all of the necessities of our daily lives, especially for the corn. The groom

also designs the bride's jewellery and shoes – the latter have to be made from the hide of an animal he has hunted himself. The shoes for the bride may only fit her feet. We also admired the pearls shown to us by the Hopi and the wonderful jewellery they make from turqoise. We were very impressed with the craftsmanship and the pride with which their culture was presented as we learned of an interesting recycling project the Hopi are realizing for a major hotel chain. One of the resulting products, pencils made from old hotel uniforms, was given to us. "We don't throw anything away" – this motto was hardly new to us quilters, but: this hotel management looked for and found a way of putting the special talents of the Indians to use for their future. They measure the quality of the air and water. They are replanting old, forgotten plants and herbs and exploring their properties. This particular project resulted in gardens of dream-like beauty.

You are certainly familiar with the Navajos' fame for working on the construction of the highest sky-scrapers or the furthest oil-pipelines – these people have a unique talent for understanding and working in such extreme situations and often provide the majority of the work for such projects.

"We think of the whole, not just of the moment". When the days get shorter they live a season of meditation and remembering their ancestors; when the days get longer again and the sun moves from east to west, they live in the rythms dictated by nature. All life after death enters the "spirit realm" which, continuously reborn in man and animals, is revered.

After having brought our knowledge about Native Americans up to date with visits and lectures, we found ourselves sitting across the table from them not knowing where to start. Our differences in clothing immediately catch our eye. We are dressed like most Americans, the Indian women in long skirts and dresses, mostly in turqoise. They are also wearing their unique turqoise jewellery, and the different tribes are only to be distinguished by the different colours they wear.

The pious prayer of a medicine man stops us before a traditional meal is served: freshly made pita bread, beans, chicken, ground beef, tomatoes and onions. Very soon the initial shyness has been overcome and we are laughing together about the different prejudices we confide to each other. They tell us, for example, that they thought a

Germans drink out of huge beer mugs and want to know where our husbands go hunting. Naturally we talk about our children and grandchildren and soon photos are passed around and admired as if we had all been family for years.

But what really brought us together in the end was doing patchwork and quilting together. In a workshop together, we all sewed a little mini quilt with one of their well-known mystical symbols, the "Kokopelli".

It is the stylized image of a flute player with a sort of back-pack full of positive energy. A symbol of the "bag of presents", the seeds of plants and flowers, he brings each spring. With his flute he melts the last of the winter's snow. He is a symbol for fertility, and also responsible for rain and for all that grows. It is a symbol known to many different tribes and therefore well-adapted to our workshop. We all sew Kokopellis onto our landscape designs as the Indian women tell us in their own words what the symbol means to them. In the colours of the local landscape and decorated with pebbles or pearls found outside, they are fascinating to us.

From the outside, we might have looked like any group of women anywhere on the planet working on a sewing project together, but our curiosity was awakened. Slowly, we got to know each other well, always with a sense of humour and a growing sense of respect for each other.

Our laughter, which still rings in my ears, the fun we had with our creations and the different fabrics and materials, sharing the sewing machines and the warm and friendly atmosphere – just that made the trip worthwhile.

We said good-bye with big hugs, and as one of the older Indian ladies announced "we will meet again" while pointing at the sky, I knew that meetings such as these are beauty that comes from the inside and then grows stronger, just as the Indian women had taught us.

To sew your own Kokopelli, simply transfer the design of this ever-popular flute-player to your fabric and include him in your quilt. With his performance, he will certainly bring joy to anyone looking at your quilt.

Project

Flic Flac for Beginners

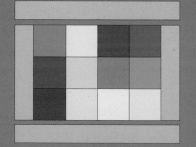

Easy and precise creation of amazing patterns – with these templates it will work like magic. You will be surprised at how quickly you manage to make complex designs, how many new ideas you will have – and how much fun it is. In the appendix, you will find five different size sets of Flic-Flac templates for the simple and double Flic-Flac, as well as for the Flic-Flac with a 14° angle.

Some basics:
All instructions are based on a 6 mm (1/4") seam allowance. The seam allowance is included in the templates. You can simply cut along the edges of templates with your small rotary cutter. When sewing pieces together make sure that you align their edges exactly and sew leaving 6 mm (1/4") seam allowance from the edge.

Preparation:
In order to avoid any sliding of the templates on your fabric, you can glue small rectangular pieces of sandpaper to the bottom sides. The sandpaper stickers have another advantage: you will never use the template upside down by mistake.

First project, getting a feel for Flic-Flac:
Cut 12 squares using the biggest template from one of the sets. Lay them out and arrange them according to your taste. Sew together the rows first, then join the rows to each other.
Turn over the finished rectangle and iron the seam allowances, one row to the left, the next to the right.
Cut border strips the width of the Flic-Flac template. Add these to the rectangle, first the short sides, then the long sides. Iron the seam allowances.
Here comes the trick: place the Flic-Flac template so that the lines marked on it fall exactly onto the first cross of seams. You will see completely new patterns start to form immediately! You can cut out the square using a small rotary cutter to cut along the edges of the template. Be careful – don't cut too far beyond the corner of the template, or you might cut into the next square!

As an alternative, you can also mark all the squares with a marker and then cut them out with scissors. The small left-over squares can be kept for a different project or be used as border or corner pieces.
Arrange the freshly cut squares in their original colour order (you will easily recognize the squares). Then give each piece a slight turn, always in the same direction.

Make sure that you see "wind-mills" made of one colour appearing, as in the picture. The Flic-Flac design is almost ready now...
Sew the squares together, first in rows, then the rows to a rectangle.
Finally you can sew a border onto the rectangle or add other Flic-Flac rectangles to it.

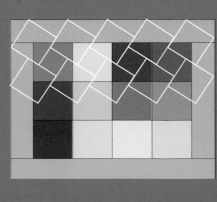

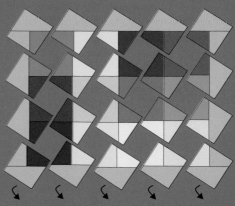

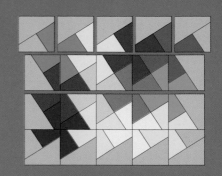

61

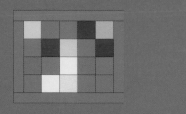

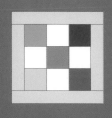 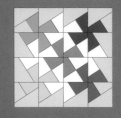

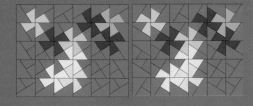

Advanced Flic-Flac

If you have successfully completed the first project, here is a list of other ideas you might try. Experiment: make pillows, handbags, quilts using your favorite fabrics. The Flic-Flac pattern is so versatile that I am sure you will discover many other variations!

Cutting some of the squares from the same fabric as the border produces an interesting effect. Like a sea of flowers the "windmills" seem to float on the background.

By the way: if you use the Flic-Flac template on the backside of your first rectangle (like working with a mirror image) you will achieve basically the same result, but with the windmills turning the other way.

If you start by laying out the elements to make big squares instead of rectangles the resulting pieces will easily combine with each other or interspersed with solid squares.

Also experiment with prints. Stripes work very well – large prints seem to work best when used sparingly and purposefully. One rule always applies: your taste decides!

The arrangement of the squares at the beginning determines the finished design. As you see in the drawing, the order of colours remains the same, but the squares become windmills.

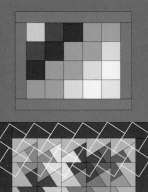

You can achieve a totally different effect by turning the cut-out pieces to the left instead of the right. In place of the windmills, you will see this kaleidoscopic pattern.

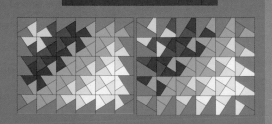

Another fascinating design is **the double Flic-Flac.** Again, you begin with simple squares to create a lively, striking design. And it isn't anywhere near as complicated as it looks!
You need to start with big squares for this design (size A or B).

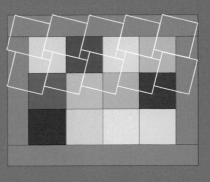

Follow the instructions to make a basic Flic-Flac. Then add another border. Don't hesitate to use a new colour, it will give even more life to the design.
Now again cut Flic-Flac squares out of the resulting rectangle using the correct size Flic-Flac template: if you started with A squares you now need the Flic-Flac template from the C set, if you started with B squares you now need the D Flic-Flac template.

Sew the resulting pieces together as before – and obtain this unique pattern!

Save the small, cut-out squares. You can use them for other projects in matching colours.

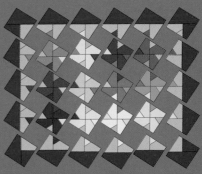

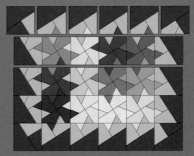

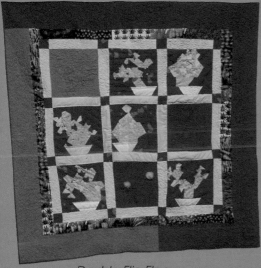

Double Flic Flac

The cacti were copied onto fabric

63

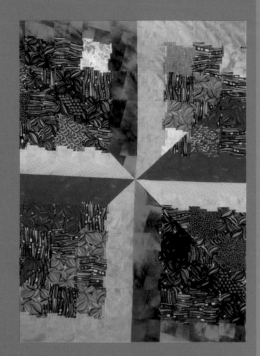

Flic-Flac 14° angle

By changing the cutting angle, you obtain completely different variations. For this reason, I have developed a Flic-Flac template with a 14° angle. You use it in the same way as the basic Flic-Flac. Here, too, you can achieve interesting results with a second cutting

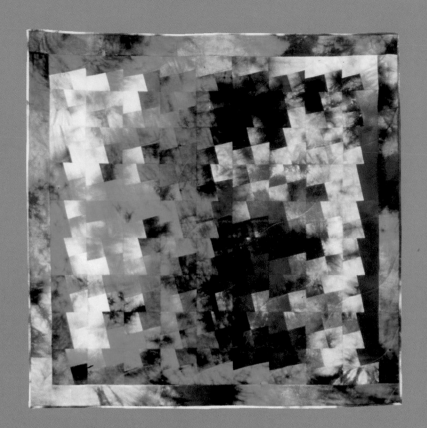

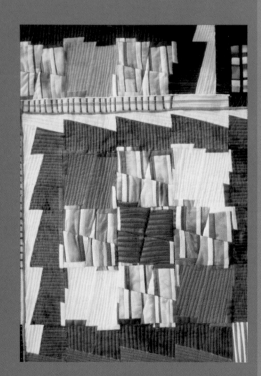

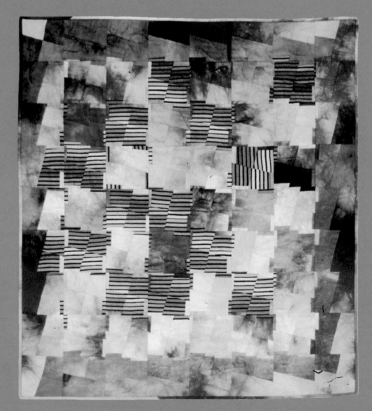

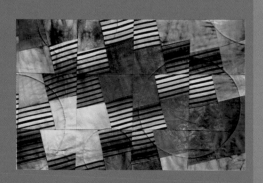

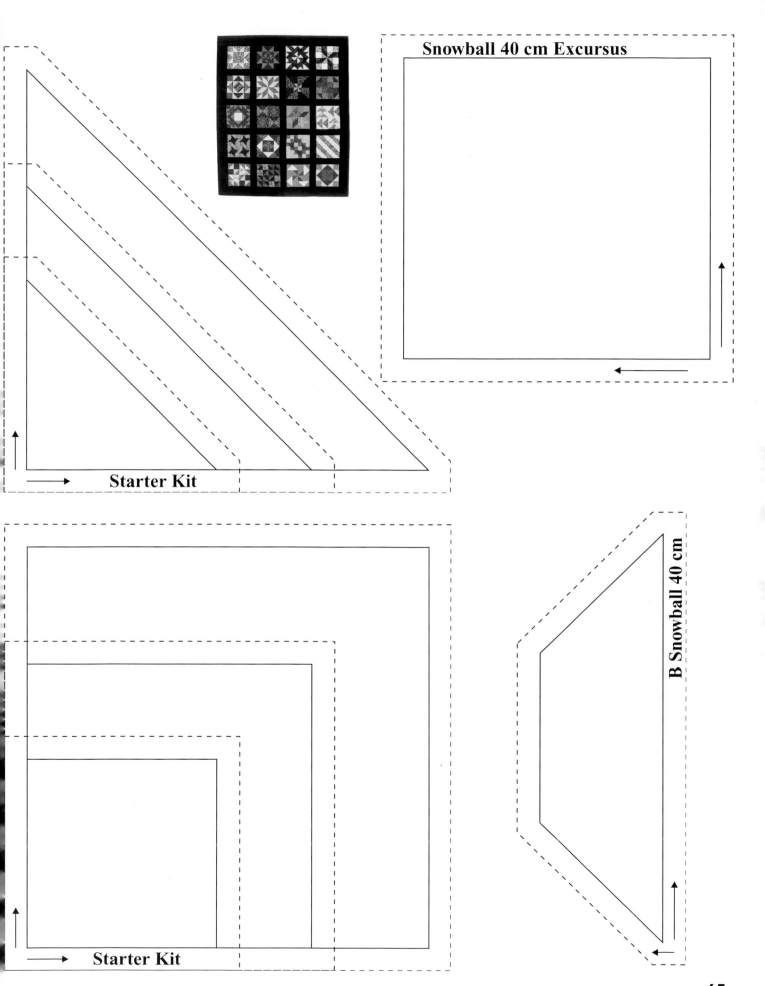

Snowball 40 cm Excursus

Starter Kit

Starter Kit

B Snowball 40 cm

65

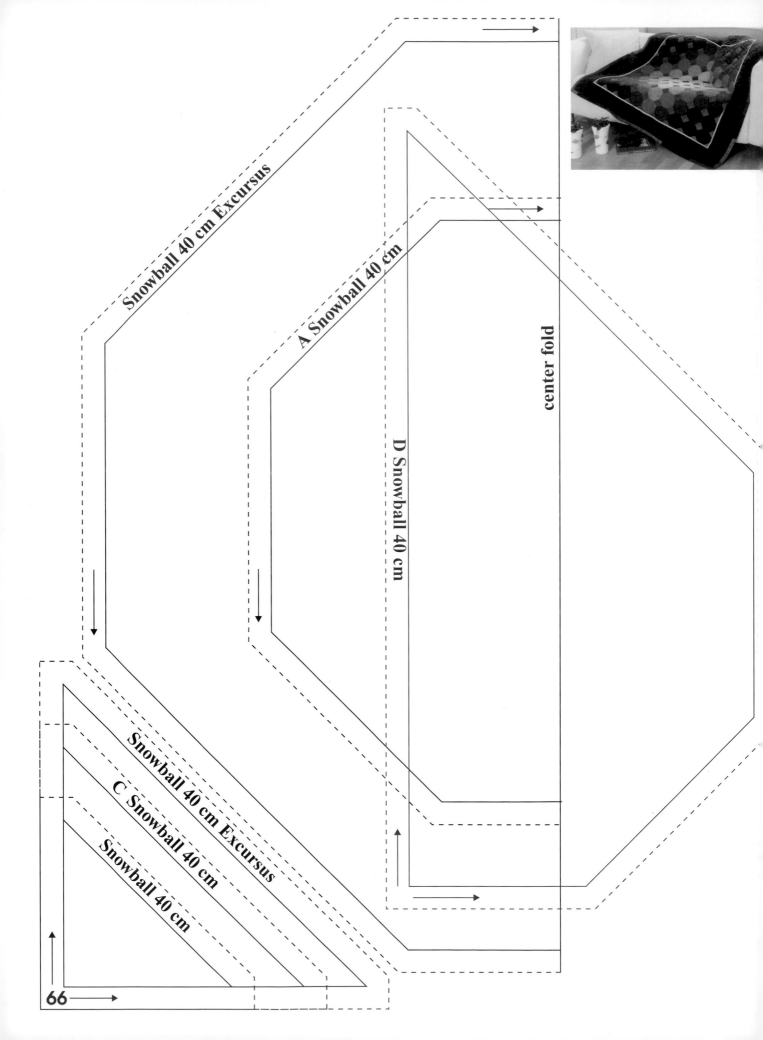

Snowball 40 cm Excursus

A Snowball 40 cm

D Snowball 40 cm

center fold

Snowball 40 cm Excursus

C Snowball 40 cm

Snowball 40 cm

66

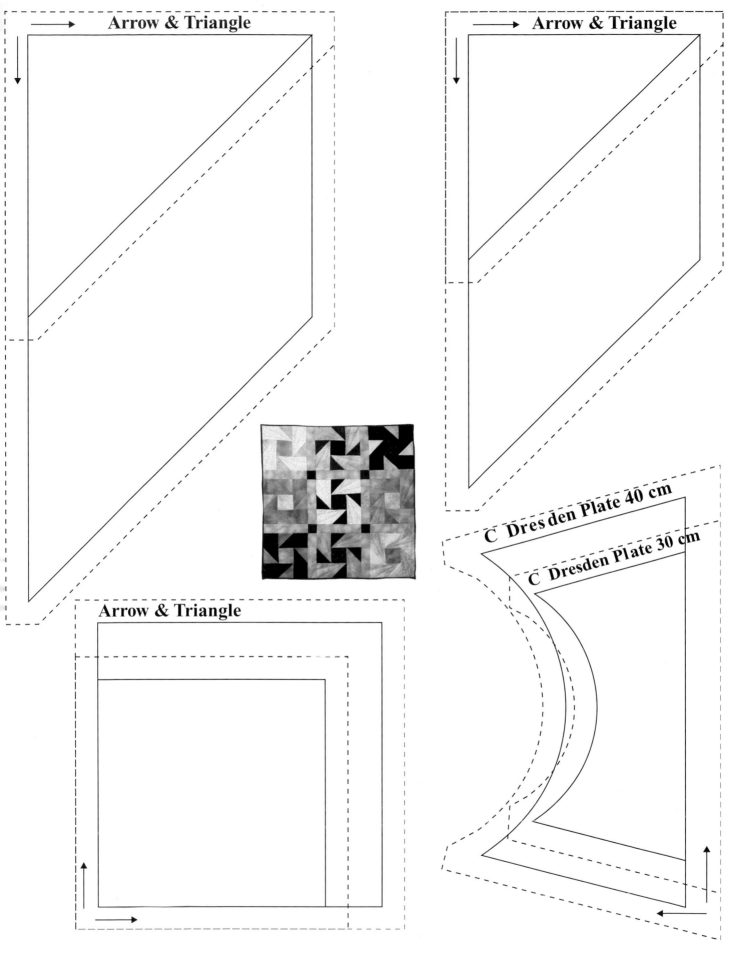

Arrow & Triangle

Arrow & Triangle

Arrow & Triangle

C Dresden Plate 40 cm

C Dresden Plate 30 cm

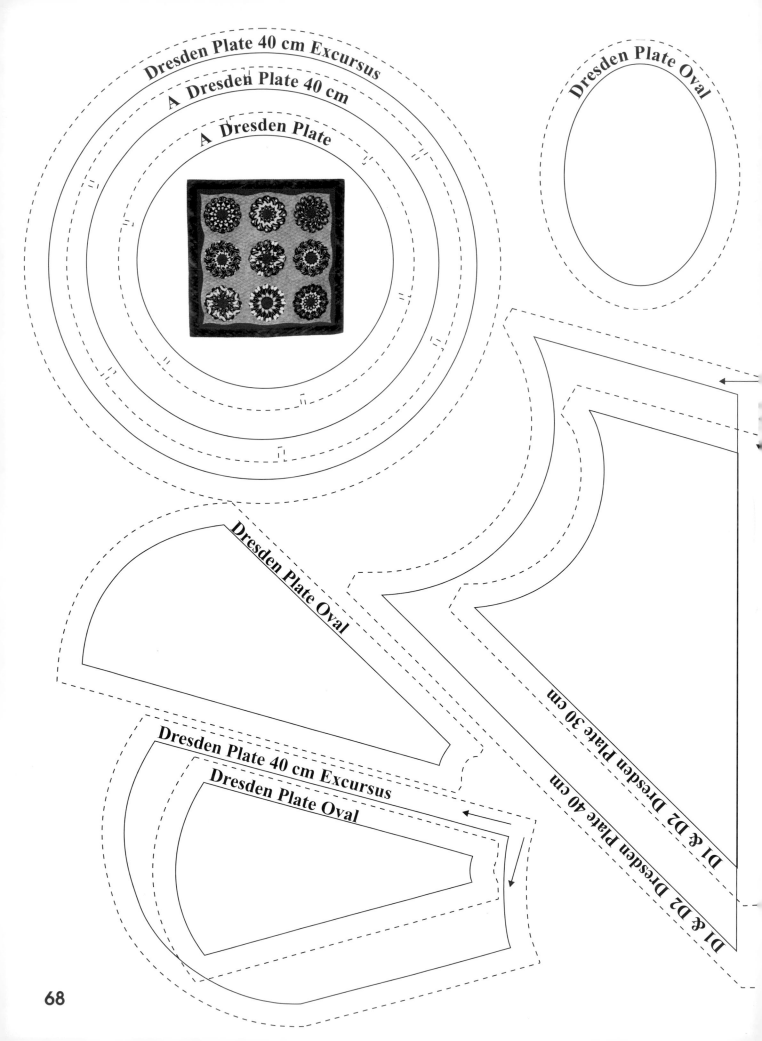

Dresden Plate 40 cm Excursus

A Dresden Plate 40 cm

A Dresden Plate

Dresden Plate Oval

Dresden Plate Oval

Dresden Plate 40 cm Excursus

Dresden Plate Oval

D1 & D2 Dresden Plate 30 cm

D1 & D2 Dresden Plate 40 cm

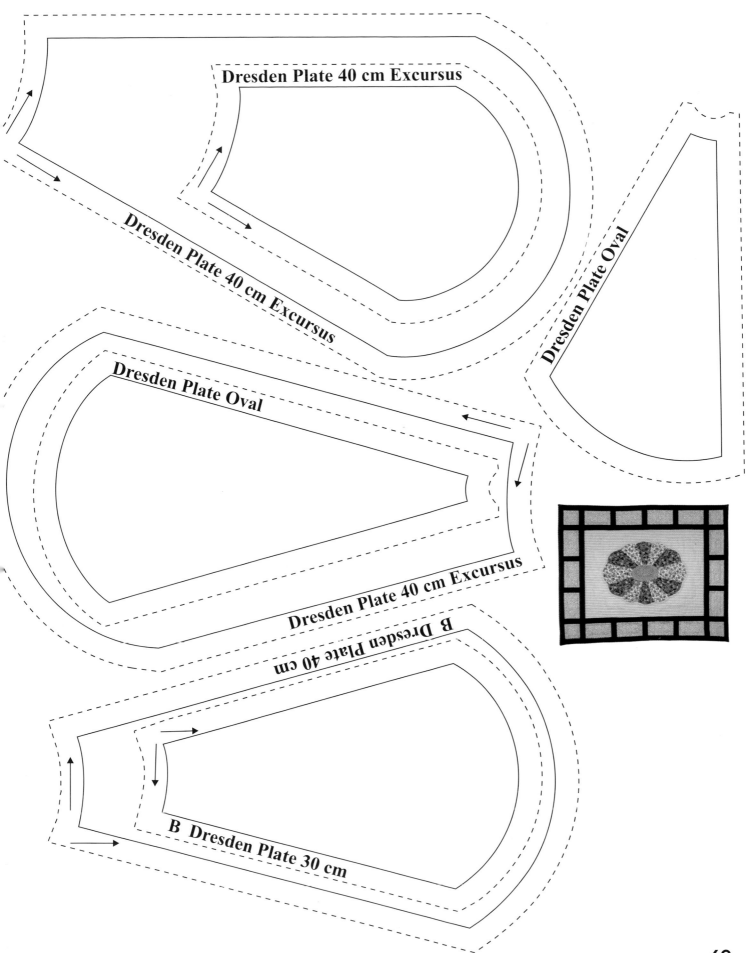

Dresden Plate 40 cm Excursus

Dresden Plate 40 cm Excursus

Dresden Plate Oval

Dresden Plate Oval

Dresden Plate 40 cm Excursus

B Dresden Plate 40 cm

B Dresden Plate 30 cm

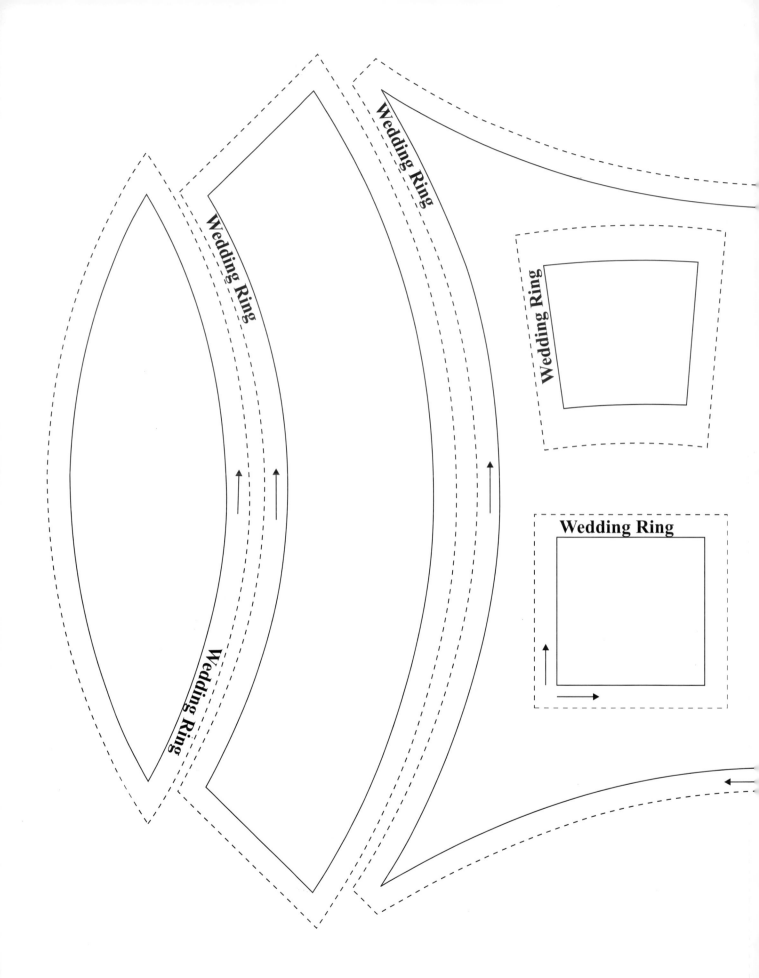

Wedding Ring

Wedding Ring

Wedding Ring

Wedding Ring

Wedding Ring

Wedding Ring

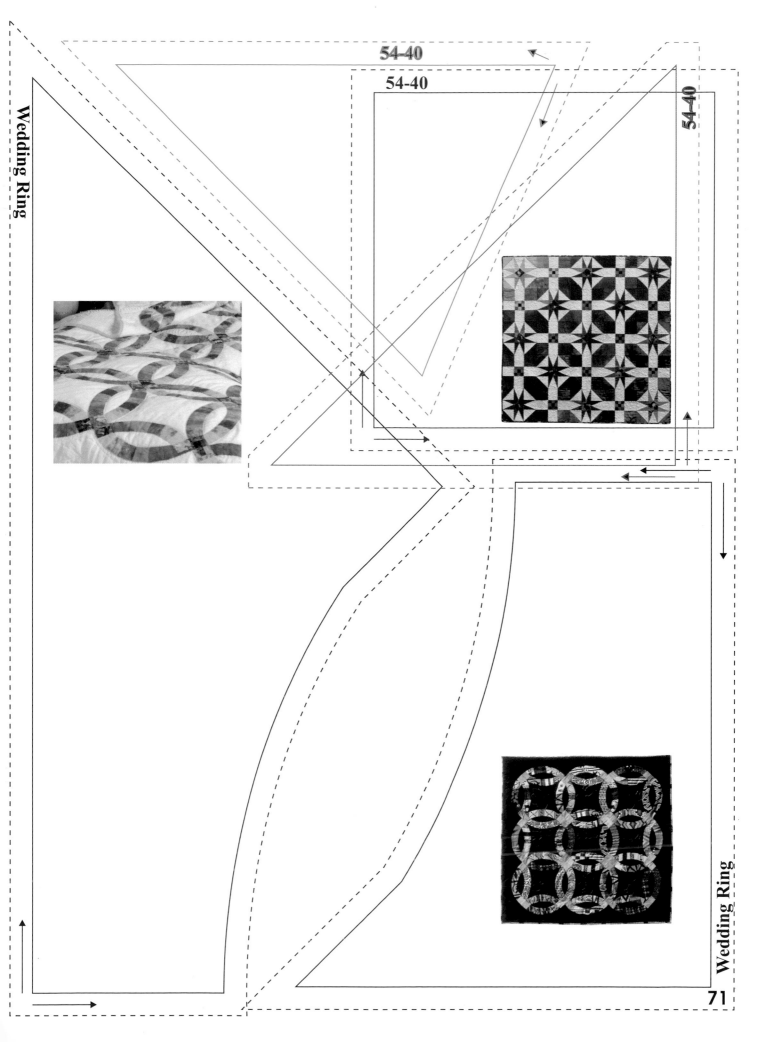

54-40

54-40

54-40

Wedding Ring

Wedding Ring

71

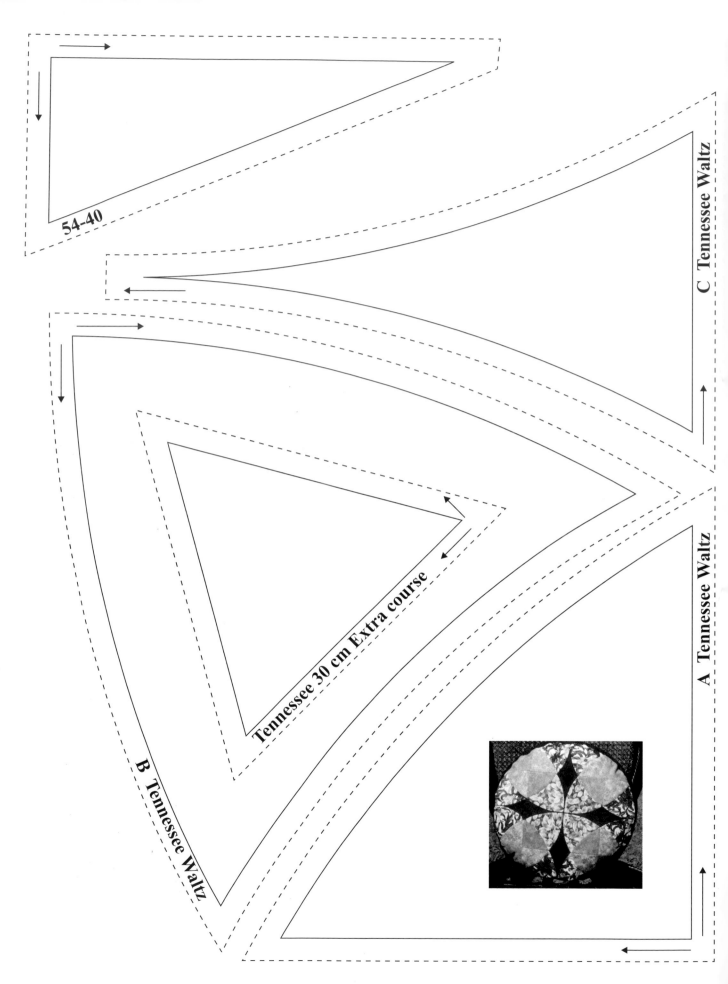

54-40

C Tennessee Waltz

Tennessee 30 cm Extra course

B Tennessee Waltz

A Tennessee Waltz

72

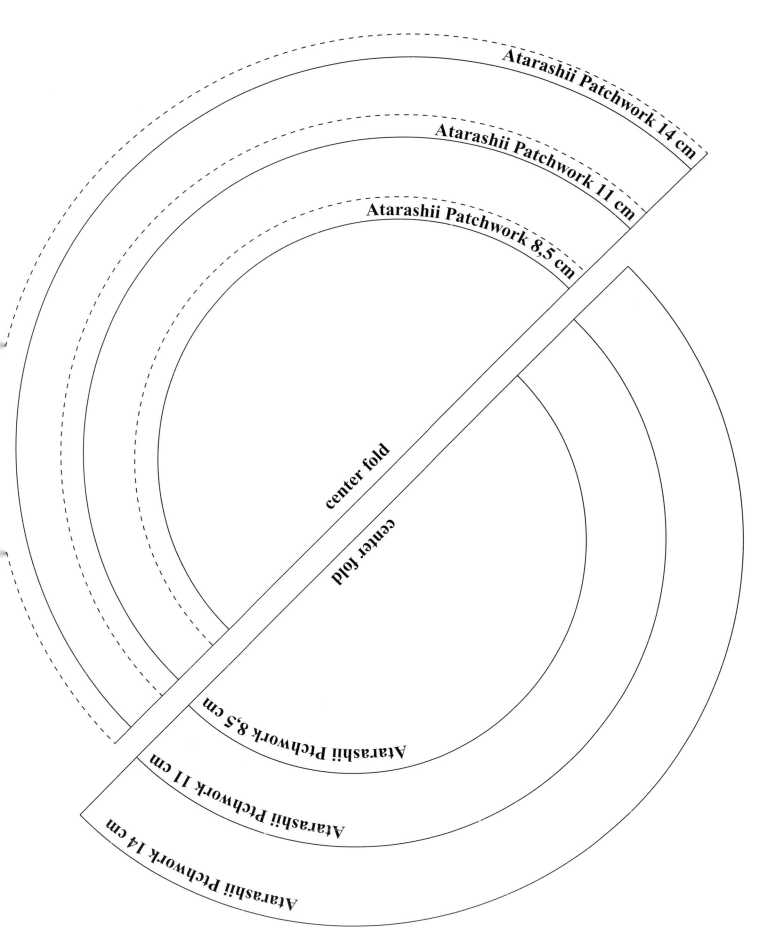

Atarashii Patchwork 14 cm

Atarashii Patchwork 11 cm

Atarashii Patchwork 8,5 cm

center fold

center fold

Atarashii Patchwork 8,5 cm

Atarashii Patchwork 11 cm

Atarashii Patchwork 14 cm

Atarashii Patchwork 14 cm

Atarashii Patchwork 11 cm

Atarashii 8,5 cm

Babyblock in rows

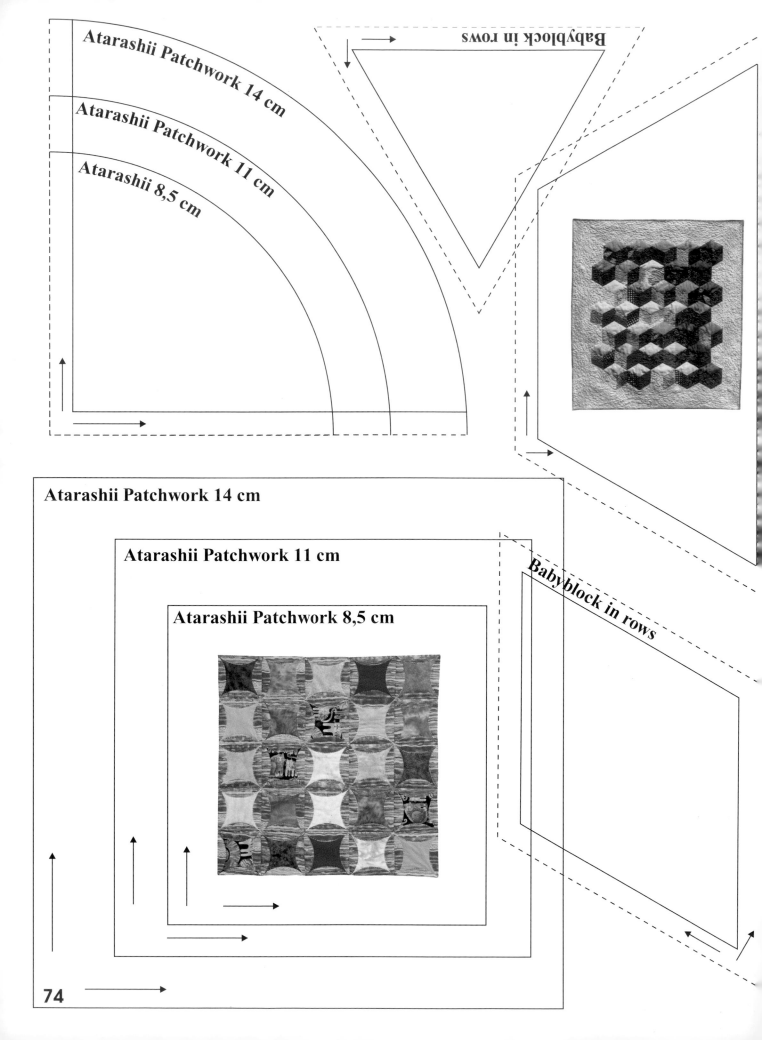

Atarashii Patchwork 14 cm

Atarashii Patchwork 11 cm

Atarashii Patchwork 8,5 cm

Babyblock in rows

Mirror Mambo – Windmill

Mirror Mambo – Windmill

Mirror Mambo 60°

Mirror Mambo 60°

Mirror Mambo 60°

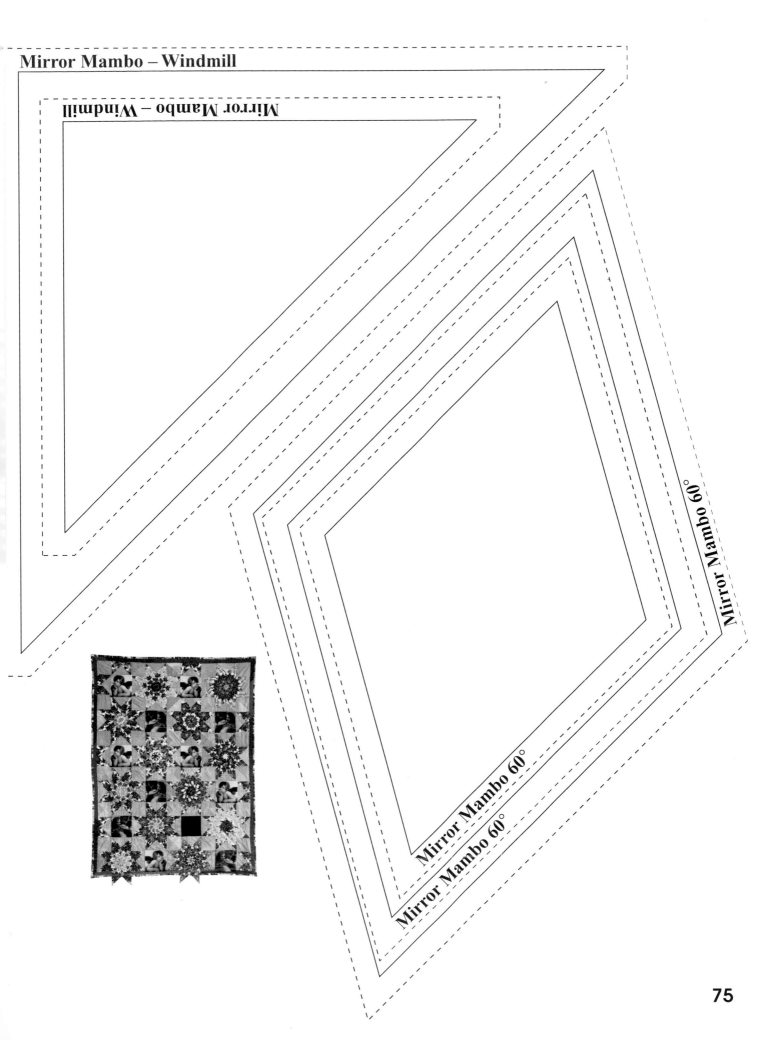

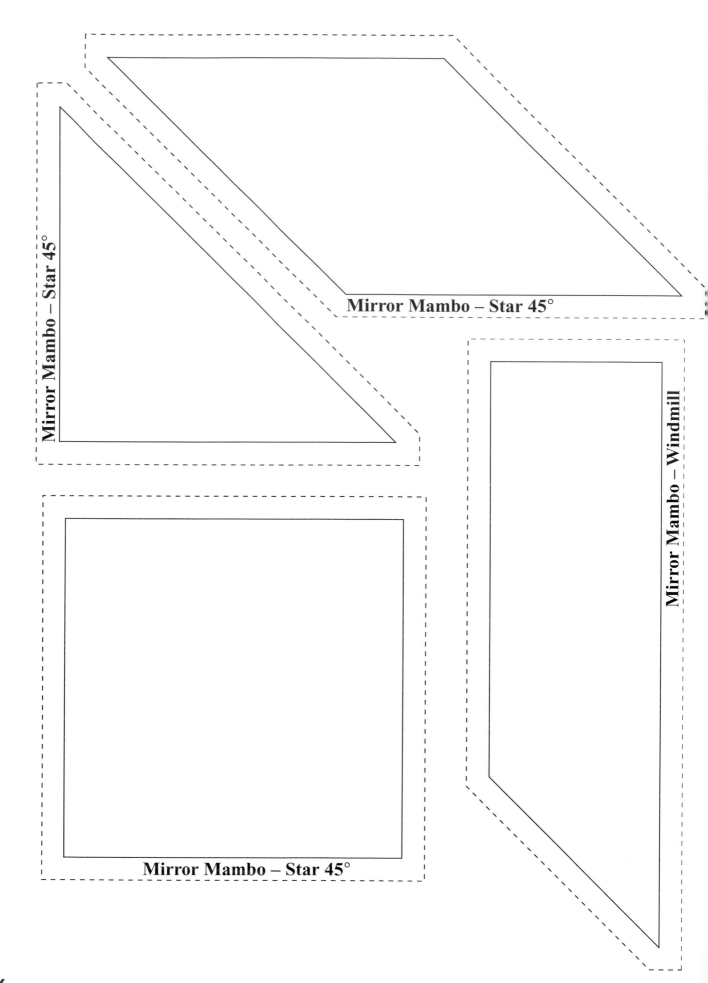

Mirror Mambo – Star 45°

Mirror Mambo – Star 45°

Mirror Mambo – Windmill

Mirror Mambo – Star 45°

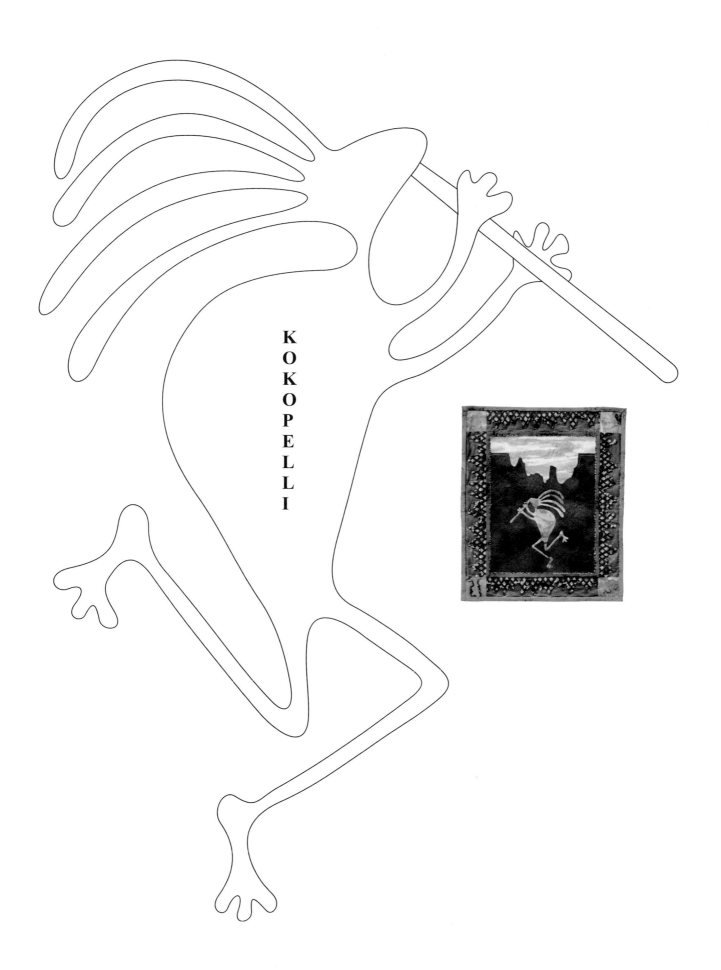

KOKOPELLI

A

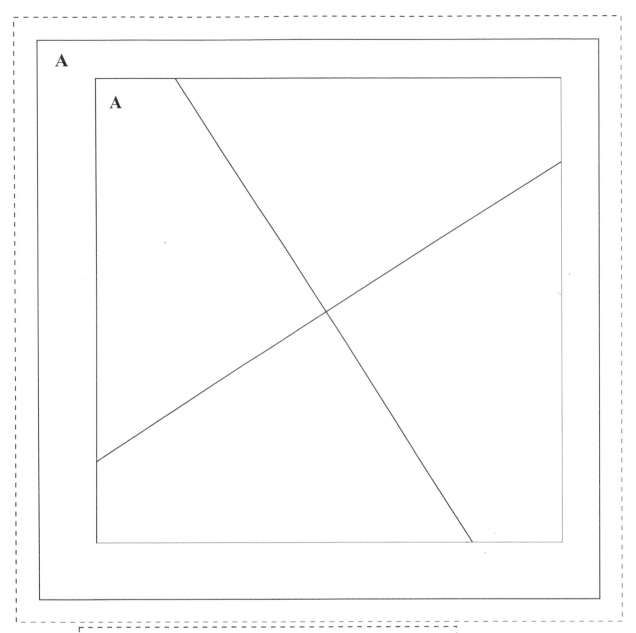

A

Flic Flac

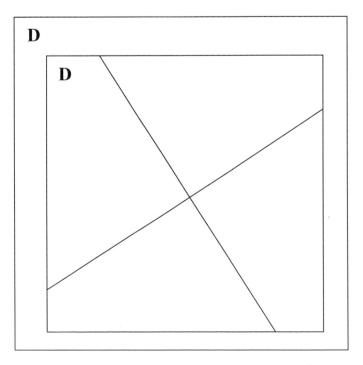

D

D

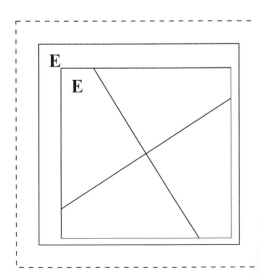

E

E

78

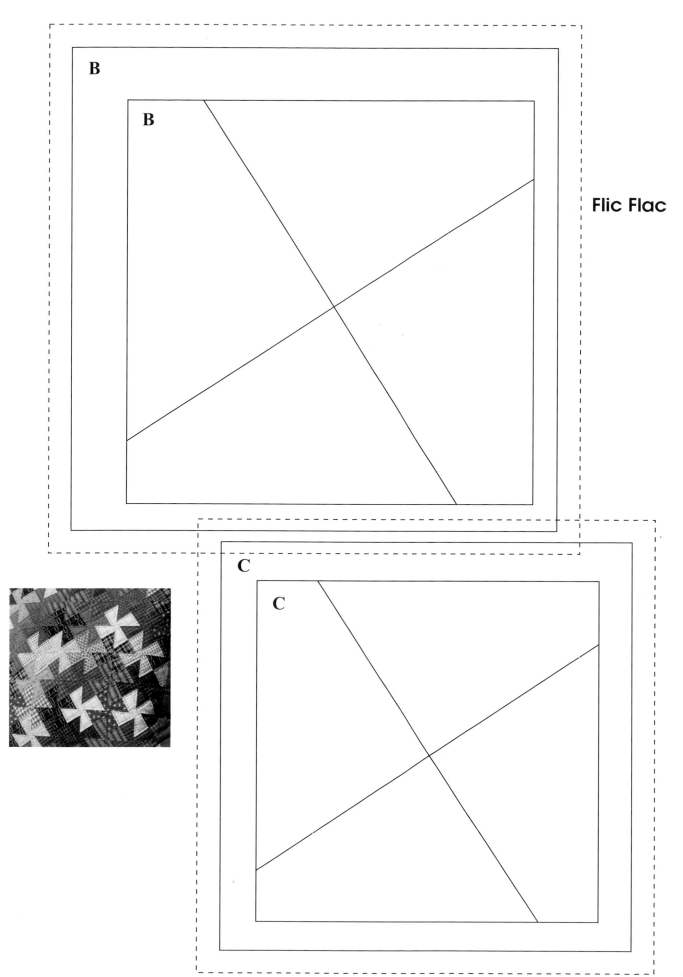

B

B

Flic Flac

C

C

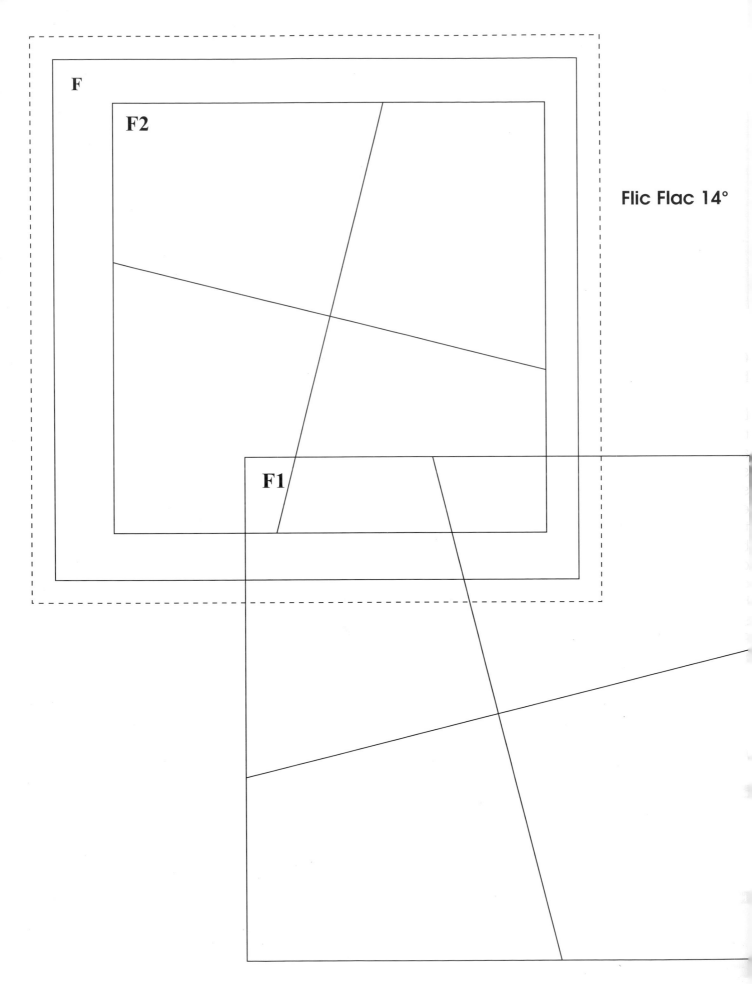

Flic Flac 14°

F

F2

F1